# REDEMPTION ROAD

*NAVIGATING MENTAL HEALTH AND SELF-CARE*
*AFTER INCARCERATION OR ADDICTION*

SEEMA DIWAN

## DISCLAIMER

This book, "Redemption Road: Navigating Mental Health and Self-Care after Incarceration or Addiction," is intended for informational and educational purposes only. The contents are not intended to substitute for professional medical advice, diagnosis, or treatment. Always seek the advice of your physician or other qualified health provider with any questions you may have regarding a medical condition or mental health disorder. Never disregard professional medical advice or delay in seeking it because of something you have read in this book.

# TABLE OF CONTENTS

# INTRODUCTION

The journey of redemption is a path many of us find ourselves on, not by choice but by the circumstances of life that have tested us beyond our limits. "Redemption Road" is more than just a book; it's a companion for those who have faced the shadows of incarceration or addiction and are striving to find their way back to light. The essence of this journey is not found in the avoidance of struggle but in the courage to confront it, the strength to overcome it, and the wisdom to grow from it.

This book is a collection of insights, stories, and guiding lights for navigating the turbulent waters of mental health and self-care after such life-altering experiences. Here, we delve deep into the human psyche, unravelling the complexities of healing and transformation that wait on the other side of hardship. It's a narrative woven from the shared experiences of individuals who have trodden this path before you. It offers relatable and poignant lessons on the power of resilience and the beauty of second chances.

Every chapter of "Redemption Road" is designed to touch a different facet of the recovery journey, from the haunting echoes of the past to the hopeful horizons of the future. We explore the depth of shame, the strength found in vulnerability, and the essence of resilience. Through creativity, relationship-building, and self-care, this book aims to guide you toward finding purpose, meaning, and a sense of community on your path to redemption.

As you turn these pages, remember that recovery is not a straight path. It's a journey filled with twists, turns, and unexpected discoveries. Yet, with every step forward, you're weaving your story of resilience and hope. "Redemption Road" reminds you that despite the struggles and setbacks, your journey is a testament to the power of second chances and the boundless potential within you. Let this book be a guide, a friend, and a beacon of hope as you navigate your way toward inner healing and restoration, always moving forward.

# CHAPTER 1

## THE WEIGHT OF THE PAST

The lingering effects of past trauma can profoundly impact one's mental health, casting a long shadow over the process of healing and recovery. When we speak of trauma, mainly stemming from experiences like incarceration or addiction, we're not just talking about memories or specific events. We're delving into a complex interplay of emotional, psychological, and physical responses that can fundamentally alter an individual's life.

Trauma, in its essence, disrupts the normal functioning of our mind and body. It's akin to a wound that, even after it has closed, leaves its mark on the surface and deep within. For many, the journey post-trauma is one of navigating a landscape filled with triggers that reignite pain, anxiety, and depression, turning even the most mundane moments into challenges. The brain, in its attempt to protect, can become overly vigilant, making relaxation and trust elusive states to achieve.

Understanding this, it becomes clear that the impact of trauma extends beyond the event itself, influencing behaviour, relationships, and even one's sense of identity. Individuals may be caught in a cycle of negative thoughts and emotions, where feelings of worthlessness, guilt, or shame become constant companions. These emotional states hinder one's ability to move forward and isolate them, making it difficult to seek or accept help.

Moreover, trauma can manifest physically, with symptoms such as insomnia, chronic pain, or unexplained medical issues, adding another layer of complexity to an already daunting journey toward healing. The body remembers and often speaks through pain when words are not enough to convey the depth of one's suffering.

Healing from trauma, therefore, is not a straightforward path. It necessitates a holistic strategy that takes care of the body, mind, and soul. The creation of coping mechanisms that can assist control trauma symptoms and provide one a sense of emotional state management is essential to this process. Amidst elevated stress or worry, methods like mindfulness, deep breathing, and grounding exercises can provide prompt alleviation.

Emotional-behavioral treatment (EMDR) and cognitive-behavioral therapy (CBT) are two examples of therapeutic therapies that have been shown to be successful in assisting people in processing and overcoming traumatic events. These therapies provide a secure environment in which a person may delve into the depths of their trauma, comprehend its effects, and progressively lessen its influence on their lives.

Creating a network of support is another essential component of recovery. Making connections with people who have gone through comparable struggles can reduce feelings of loneliness and offer a supportive and understanding group. These connections remind individuals they are not alone in their struggle, offering hope and encouragement on the more challenging days.

The journey of healing from trauma involves reclaiming one's identity beyond the scars of past experiences. It's about learning to redefine oneself not by what has happened but by the strength and resilience shown in the face of adversity. This process of self-discovery and acceptance is perhaps the most challenging yet rewarding aspect of healing, as it opens the door to a life defined not by trauma but by the possibilities of the present and future.

In essence, the path to recovery from past trauma is intricate and deeply personal. It requires endurance, bravery, and a readiness to confront one's worst fears. Nonetheless, there is room for significant personal development and transformation on this trip, which is evidence of the resilience of the human spirit.

## Real-life example

Sarah's journey into the depths of her psyche began not at the moment of her release from prison but in the silent aftermath that followed. Once the gates closed behind her, she entered a world vastly different from what she remembered. The freedom she longed for during her incarceration became a source of overwhelming anxiety and depression, painting her days in shades of grey she struggled to navigate.

The walls of her cell were no longer there, but invisible barriers built from her fears and memories seemed just as confining. Sarah found herself haunted by the stigma of her past, a label that felt like a shadow she couldn't shake. Each day brought with it the challenge of facing a society that often looked upon her with suspicion and judgment, making her journey of reintegration an uphill battle.

Anxiety became a constant companion for Sarah, manifesting in sleepless nights and days filled with unrest. Social situations, once a source of joy, now felt like minefields. She was perpetually on edge, constantly bracing for judgment or rejection. Depression soon followed a heavy blanket that dulled her experiences and made even the simplest tasks seem impossible. The world outside, with its bright colours and bustling life, contrasted sharply with the darkness that seemed to envelop her.

Sarah's story, however, doesn't end in despair. Recognizing the depth of her struggle, she reached out for help, a step that required all the courage she had left. Therapy introduced her to tools and strategies to manage her anxiety and depression, offering a glimmer of hope in her darkest moments. Through cognitive-behavioral therapy, she began to challenge and reframe the negative thoughts that had taken root in her mind, learning to separate her identity from her past.

Support groups played a crucial role in Sarah's healing process. Meeting others who shared similar experiences gave her a sense of belonging and understanding that she had long craved. These connections reminded her that she was not alone, that her feelings were valid, and that healing was indeed possible.

Slowly, Sarah started rebuilding her life, brick by brick. She found solace in art, channelling her emotions into paintings that told her story in colors and strokes. Each piece was a step towards healing, a tangible expression of her inner journey. Sarah also volunteered, finding purpose in helping others, which, in turn, helped diminish her feelings of worthlessness and isolation.

Sarah's story demonstrates how the human spirit can persevere in the face of difficulty. It serves as a reminder that there is more than one way to recover, that obstacles must be overcome, and that asking for assistance is a show of strength rather than weakness. Through her courage to face her anxiety and depression head-on, Sarah has begun to weave a new tapestry for her life, one that includes the dark threads of her past but also the bright colors of her newfound hope and strength.

# CHAPTER 2

## BREAKING THE CHAINS OF SHAME

S tigma is like a shadow that follows individuals long after they've served their time in prison or taken the brave steps to overcome addiction. This social stigma, deeply rooted in misunderstanding and prejudice, can significantly impact the lives of those trying to rebuild and move forward. It's a barrier that often stands between them and a second chance at life, affecting their mental health, job opportunities, and relationships.

Imagine carrying a label invisible to you but glaringly visible to society, a label that screams "former inmate" or "addict," regardless of the person you've become or the strides you've made towards recovery. This is the daily reality for many people coming out of incarceration or addiction recovery. They are met with skepticism and mistrust, making their journey towards reintegration an uphill battle. The stigma attached to their pasts constantly reminds them of their lowest moments, overshadowing their accomplishments and growth.

The impact of this stigma is profound. It isolates individuals, making them feel unworthy of support or a second chance. Many struggle in silence, fearing judgment or rejection if they seek help. This seclusion can worsen mental health conditions like anxiety and despair, entangling sufferers in a vicious cycle that can be difficult to escape. For those recovering from addiction, the fear of stigma can deter them from seeking the treatment they need, increasing the risk of relapse.

Furthermore, stigma can close doors to essential opportunities for rebuilding a life. Finding employment can be a daunting task when a criminal record or a history of addiction makes employers hesitant to offer a job. Housing, too, can become an obstacle, with many landlords unwilling to rent to someone with a past they don't understand. These societal barriers can seem impossible, leaving individuals feeling defeated and marginalized.

Yet, it's essential to recognize that the stigma surrounding incarceration and addiction is based on stereotypes and fear, not reality. People are not defined by their lowest points. Growth and change are always possible. The journey of recovery and rehabilitation is a testament to human resilience and strength. It's a path marked by hard-won victories, lessons learned, and a gradual reclamation of identity beyond the confines of past mistakes.

Breaking down the walls of stigma requires a collective effort. It starts with conversations that challenge our preconceptions and biases. It involves educating ourselves and others about the realities of incarceration and addiction, highlighting the human stories behind the statistics. By fostering empathy and understanding, we can dismantle the barriers that stigma creates.

Communities play a crucial role in this process. Supportive communities that offer acceptance and opportunities can make all the difference in someone's recovery journey. Programs that focus on reintegration and rehabilitation rather than punishment show promising results in reducing recidivism and aiding recovery from addiction. These initiatives help individuals rebuild their lives and benefit society as a whole.

Moreover, individuals who have navigated these challenges can be powerful advocates for change. By sharing their stories, they illuminate the possibility of redemption and the capacity for transformation. They remind us that everyone deserves compassion, respect, and the opportunity to make a new start.

The stigma surrounding incarceration and addiction is a significant hurdle for many trying to rebuild their lives. It's a societal issue that calls for understanding, empathy, and action. By challenging our perceptions and fostering supportive communities, we can help break the cycle of stigma and isolation. Together, we can create a more inclusive society where second chances are not just possible but embraced as opportunities for growth and transformation.

## Real-life example

John's story is a testament to the human spirit's resilience in the face of addiction and the harsh judgment of society. Growing up in a small town, John was introduced to drugs in his teenage years, a decision that spiralled into a decade-long battle with addiction. It wasn't just the addiction that John had to fight; it was the stigma attached to it, a stigma that branded him in the eyes of his community and, at times, even in his own eyes.

John's journey to recovery began with the realization that his life had become unmanageable. The moment of truth came one cold evening when he found himself alone, grappling with the consequences of his addiction. Then, he decided to seek help, which marked the first step on his long road to self-acceptance.

Entering a rehabilitation program, John was confronted with the total weight of his addiction, not only its physical grip but its emotional and psychological hold. Recovery was far from easy. Every day, he presented a new challenge, from the physical withdrawal symptoms to the deep-seated feelings of guilt and shame that had accumulated over the years.

Yet, as John navigated the path to sobriety, he also began to tackle the societal judgment that came with being a recovering addict. In his community, addiction was often seen as a moral failing rather than a disease, a viewpoint that left him feeling ostracized and misunderstood. Despite these challenges, John remained steadfast in his commitment to recovery, driven by a growing sense of self-awareness and a desire to redefine his life on his terms.

One of the most significant hurdles John faced was rebuilding his identity beyond his addiction. He had to learn to see himself not as society saw him but as someone worthy of respect and compassion. This process of self-acceptance was nurtured through therapy, support groups, and sharing his story with others. In doing so, John discovered that his experiences could offer hope and guidance to those walking a similar path.

John's journey was not just about overcoming addiction; it was about confronting and overcoming the societal stigma that so often shadows recovery. He became an advocate for change, speaking out against the misconceptions surrounding addiction and working to support others in their recovery efforts. Through his actions, John has helped foster a more understanding and compassionate community that recognizes the courage it takes to face addiction and the strength it takes to overcome it.

Today, John lives a life defined not by his past struggles but by his achievements and ongoing commitment to helping others. His story is a powerful reminder that recovery is possible and societal judgment can be transformed into societal support. John's journey to self-acceptance after battling addiction and societal judgment is a beacon of hope for anyone facing the darkness of addiction, proving that with determination, support, and a willingness to confront stigma, a new chapter of life can begin.

# CHAPTER 3

## EMBRACING VULNERABILITY

Opening ourselves up to others, showing our true feelings, and admitting our fears and weaknesses might seem scary. We often think it makes us look weak or that others might use our openness against us. However, vulnerability is one of the most incredible forces for healing and creating deep connections with others we can experience. It's about letting down our guards and showing who we are, which can lead to genuine understanding and support from those around us.

Being vulnerable doesn't mean sharing our deepest secrets with everyone we meet. It's about being honest with ourselves and those we trust, allowing us to be seen, flaws and all. This honesty opens the door to healing, as it confronts us with our true selves, not the version we often pretend to be to fit in or to hide our pain. In the process, we learn that our imperfections are not reasons for shame but are part of what makes us human.

For many, the journey toward embracing vulnerability starts with acknowledging their struggles. It could be the struggles of dealing with a brutal past, facing mental health issues, or overcoming personal failures. When we start talking about these parts of our lives, especially those we're not proud of, we take the first step in healing. We often find that sharing our stories not only lightens our load but can also help others feel less alone in their battles.

One of the most beautiful aspects of vulnerability is how it can strengthen relationships. When we open up to someone, we permit them to do the same, creating a space where deep, meaningful connections can flourish. These connections are based on mutual trust and understanding, forming bonds that can offer incredible support and comfort through life's ups and downs.

However, embracing vulnerability is not without its challenges. It requires courage to face potential judgment and rejection. Yet, it's important to remember that the strength of vulnerability lies not in the reaction of others but in the act itself. By choosing to be vulnerable, we assert control over our narrative, refusing to let fear dictate how we live our lives.

In a society that often values strength and self-sufficiency above all, admitting to needing help can be seen as a sign of weakness. But it's precisely in these moments of openness that true strength is shown. Asking for help from friends, family, or professionals is a brave step toward healing. It acknowledges that we are not isolated islands but part of a larger community where support and compassion are available.

Moreover, the power of vulnerability is not just in personal healing and connection but can also spark more comprehensive change. When people with influence share their struggles, it can help break down the stigma around issues like mental health, encouraging a culture of openness and support. It shows that no one is immune to challenges, fostering a more empathetic and understanding society.

In embracing vulnerability, we also find a path to self-acceptance. By accepting our flaws and imperfections, we learn to extend the same compassion to ourselves as we do to others. This self-compassion is crucial in healing, replacing self-criticism and shame with love and understanding.

The journey toward embracing vulnerability is a profoundly personal one, filled with its own set of challenges and rewards. It asks us to let go of our fears, trust in the strength of our connections, and believe in the healing power of openness. While the road may be uncertain, the destination—a life marked by genuine relationships, self-acceptance, and the freedom to be our true selves—is undoubtedly worth the journey.

## Real-life example

Maria's story unfolds like many others in the shadows of a life once constrained by incarceration, a time that left invisible scars more profound than the visible ones. Upon her release, Maria carried not only the weight of reintegrating into society but also the burden of mental health struggles that went largely unspoken. The stigma of her past and the battles within her mind created an almost palpable silence.

For years, Maria moved through her days wearing a mask of okay-ness, a facade that hid her inner turmoil. Anxiety and depression, her uninvited companions, whispered doubts and fears, making even the simplest tasks feel like insurmountable obstacles. The expectation to immediately adjust and thrive post-release only added to her sense of isolation. Maria felt trapped in a cycle of silent suffering, believing that her struggles were hers to face alone, a belief reinforced by the societal stigma surrounding both her incarceration and her mental health.

However, Maria's journey took a pivotal turn when she reached a point of exhaustion from the constant act of pretending. A quiet moment of self-reflection sparked a realization: the first step toward healing was acknowledging her need for help. This moment of vulnerability, though terrifying, was Maria's first act of courage on her path to recovery.

Opening up about her struggles marked the beginning of Maria's transformation. She started with a trusted friend, her voice shaky but determined as she shared the reality of her daily battles. The fear of judgment loomed large, but it was met with compassion and understanding, a response that surprised Maria and challenged her preconceptions about how others would react.

Emboldened by this experience, Maria sought professional help, a decision that led her to therapy, where she learned to navigate her mental health issues with guidance and support. Through treatment, she discovered tools and strategies that helped manage her anxiety and depression, offering her a sense of control for the first time in years.

Maria's openness became her strength, leading her to join support groups for individuals facing similar challenges. In these groups, she found a community of empathy and shared experiences, a space where her struggles were met with nods of understanding rather than judgment. Sharing her story, in turn, helped others feel less alone in their journeys, creating a cycle of support and understanding.

What truly stands out in Maria's story is not just her courage to seek help but her decision to use her experiences to advocate for mental health awareness within communities affected by incarceration. She began volunteering, sharing her journey at events, and working with organizations that support individuals post-incarceration. Maria transformed her pain into a powerful message: vulnerability is not a weakness but a gateway to healing and connection.

Today, Maria continues to advocate for mental health, especially highlighting the challenges faced by those re-entering society post-incarceration. Her journey from silent suffering to vocal advocacy underscores a powerful truth: opening up about one's struggles can be the most courageous step toward healing. Maria's story is a testament to the strength found in vulnerability, the importance of community support, and the transformative power of embracing one's truth.

# CHAPTER 4

## CULTIVATING RESILIENCE

**B**uilding resilience in the face of adversity is akin to fortifying a castle, preparing it to withstand sieges of all magnitudes. Resilience is not an innate trait gifted to a fortunate few but a series of strategies and behaviors that anyone can develop over time. It's about bouncing back from challenges, learning from failure, and emerging more robust and adaptable. Here are comprehensive strategies to build resilience when faced with life's inevitable storms.

### Understand and Accept Your Feelings

The first step in building resilience is acknowledging and accepting your emotions. Adversity often brings a storm of feelings — fear, anger, sadness, or even guilt. Recognize these emotions as natural responses to your circumstances. Allow yourself to feel them without judgment. Understanding your emotional reactions to challenges is crucial in developing a mindful approach to overcoming them.

### Foster Optimism

Maintaining a positive outlook in facing difficulties does not mean ignoring reality. It's about cultivating a sense of hope and confidence in your ability to cope and eventually thrive. Optimism is a cornerstone of resilience, empowering you to view setbacks as temporary and surmountable. Remind yourself of your prior achievements in conquering challenges and make a habit of searching for the bright side of challenging circumstances.

### Strengthen Your Support Network

No fortress can stand alone; it requires a strong foundation and support. Similarly, building resilience is not a solitary endeavor. Cultivate relationships with friends, family, and mentors who offer encouragement and understanding. A strong support system serves as a listening ear for your worries, a guide when you're lost, and a constant reminder that you're not the only one going through difficult times.

### Set Realistic Goals and Take Action

Resilience involves setting realistic, achievable goals and taking decisive steps toward them. Divide up your most ambitious goals into more doable, smaller activities. Every little triumph will increase your self-esteem and sense of achievement, which will motivate you to keep going.

Taking action reinforces your agency and control over your situation, no matter how small.

### Embrace Change

Adversity frequently arises from change, which is an unavoidable aspect of life. Resilient individuals understand that change is unavoidable and an opportunity for growth. Practice adaptability by setting flexible goals and remaining open to new directions and opportunities.

Embracing change rather than resisting it can transform potential stressors into avenues for personal development.

### Develop Problem-Solving Skills

When faced with a challenge, resilient people devise a plan of action. Enhance your problem-solving skills by brainstorming multiple solutions to an issue, weighing their pros and cons, and deciding on the best course of action. This proactive approach empowers you to tackle obstacles head-on rather than feeling overwhelmed.

## Foster Self-Compassion and Forgiveness

Be kind to yourself. Building resilience is as much about self-compassion as it is about toughness. Recognize that setbacks are part of the human experience and not a reflection of your worth. Accept responsibility for your errors and see them as chances to improve. Having empathy and understanding for oneself helps you develop a resilient outlook.

## Prioritize Self-Care

Resilience requires energy, both physical and emotional. Make self-care a priority by making sure you get enough sleep, eat healthily, exercise, and partake in activities that uplift your emotions. A healthy body and mind are your best defenses against the stresses of adversity.

## Seek Purpose

Finding a purpose can profoundly impact your ability to cope with challenges. Purpose gives your struggles meaning, motivating you to persevere through tough times. Having a distinct sense of purpose, whether it is through volunteering, pursuing a passion, or aiming high, may greatly increase resilience.

## Learn from the Past

Reflect on past adversities and the strategies that helped you overcome them. What strengths did you discover about yourself? What would you do differently? Gaining knowledge from prior events will boost your resilience confidence and offer insightful advice for dealing with obstacles in the future.

**Practice Mindfulness**

Two ways that mindfulness, the practice of being fully present and absorbed in the moment, might enhance resilience are by lowering stress and promoting emotional balance. In the midst of chaos, awareness may be developed by yoga, deep breathing, and meditation.

Resilience building is a process rather than a final goal. It calls for perseverance, hard work, and a dedication to one's own development. By employing these strategies, you can fortify your mental and emotional defenses, preparing you to face life's challenges with courage, grace, and unwavering strength.

## Real-life example

Alex's resilience journey began on a cold morning as he stepped out of the confines of a place that had been his reality for years. Incarceration had left its mark, not just on his record, but deep within his psyche, challenging his sense of self and his hopes for the future.

The world outside the prison gates was both familiar and utterly alien, filled with opportunities yet bristling with barriers erected by his past.

During the first few days of his release, Alex struggled with the burden of social criticism and the enormous undertaking of starting again. Employment opportunities seemed a distant dream, as every application was met with skepticism due to his incarceration history. Relationships strained under the pressure of his past, leaving him navigating a labyrinth of loneliness and misunderstanding.

Yet, Alex's resilience began to take shape within this crucible of challenges. The first step in his journey was accepting his reality, not with resignation but with the determination to change it. He recognized that while he couldn't alter his past, he had control over how he faced his future. This realization was a beacon that guided him through the darkest moments.

Small, determined steps fuelled Alex's transformation. He volunteered his time, a decision that filled his days with purpose, and slowly began to mend the fabric of his community ties.

Through volunteering, he demonstrated his commitment to positive change, gradually altering the perceptions of those around him.

Education played a crucial role in Alex's journey. He embraced learning with enthusiasm, understanding that knowledge was a key that could unlock many doors that his past had closed. Night classes and online courses became his ladder out of the pit of despair; each completed course a rung towards a new horizon.

The most significant battle Alex fought was within himself. The stigma of incarceration had left deep wounds of shame and worthlessness. Alex learned to separate his sense of self from his past actions through counseling and support groups. He discovered self-compassion and forgiveness, realizing he was more than the sum of his mistakes. This internal shift transformed his outlook on life and his place within it.

Resilience for Alex also meant facing rejection and setbacks without allowing them to define his journey. With every closed door, he sought another that might open. When employment seemed impossible, Alex created his opportunity by starting a small business. It was a humble beginning, leveraging the skills he had honed before and during his incarceration, but it was his.

The strength of the human spirit and adaptability are demonstrated by Alex's inspirational tale of perseverance. He shared his experience to encourage and assist people pursuing the same route he had, turning into a ray of hope for those dealing with comparable difficulties.

His life, once defined by the boundaries of incarceration, expanded far beyond those walls, encompassing community, achievement, and a newfound sense of self-worth.

Today, Alex's resilience has rebuilt his life and woven him back into the fabric of society as an individual who contributes, supports, and uplifts. His journey underscores the truth that adversity may shape us but does not have to confine us. Through resilience, courage, and community support, transformation is possible and within reach.

# CHAPTER 5

## FINDING PURPOSE AND MEANING

**D**iscovering purpose and meaning in life, especially after enduring setbacks or navigating the aftermath of past mistakes, is akin to finding a compass amid a storm. It provides direction, imbues our actions with significance, and offers a sense of fulfilment that transcends the immediate pleasures of daily life. This quest for purpose and meaning is not merely about achieving happiness but about anchoring oneself to something greater, which, in turn, can transform the way we view ourselves and our place in the world.

The path beyond previous errors frequently starts in the shadow of regret and remorse, feelings that may distort our judgment and make us doubt our value. However, within this introspection, the seeds of purpose can be found. A person's sense of purpose is deeply personal and can come from a variety of places, such as following hobbies, developing skills, or positively impacting the lives of others. It requires us to look beyond our experiences' surface, extract lessons from our missteps, and envision a future where those lessons guide our choices and actions.

Finding purpose is significant for manifold reasons. First, it instills a sense of stability and resilience. When a clear understanding of purpose drives our actions, we are better equipped to navigate life's ups and downs. Challenges become less about the obstacles and more about opportunities to reaffirm our commitments to our values and goals. This shift in perspective can be profoundly empowering, especially for those who have felt defined by their past mistakes.

Moreover, purpose fosters growth and self-improvement. It propels us forward, encouraging us to set goals and pursue achievements that align with our deepest values. This pursuit is not about erasing past errors but building a future where those errors no longer dictate our paths. It's about recognizing that growth is a continuous journey that is enriched, not diminished, by the lessons learned from our missteps.

Finding purpose also enhances our connections with others. We naturally align ourselves with like-minded individuals when we engage in activities or causes that resonate with our core values. These connections are not superficial but are rooted in shared aspirations and mutual support. They offer a sense of belonging that can be incredibly healing, reminding us that we are part of a larger tapestry of human experience, interconnected and interdependent.

Furthermore, purpose can be a powerful antidote to the isolation and alienation that often accompany past mistakes. It shifts the focus from what we have done to who we can become, opening doors to forgiveness — both self-forgiveness and forgiveness from others. This transition from self-condemnation to self-acceptance is crucial in healing and moving forward.

Embarking for purpose and meaning requires courage, especially in the face of societal judgment or self-doubt. It might involve exploring new interests, volunteering, returning to forgotten passions, or simply reflecting on what truly matters to us. The key is to remain open and curious, willing to take risks, and patient with ourselves as we navigate this journey.

Finding purpose and meaning beyond past mistakes is about redefining our narratives. It's about writing a new chapter in our lives, one where our past serves as a backdrop, not the defining feature of our story. This quest for purpose is liberating and grounding, offering a path to redemption marked by self-discovery, connection, and a renewed hope for the future. It is a testament to the enduring capacity for change and the resilience of the human spirit.

Real-life example

Emily's story is a journey from the depths of addiction to the discovery of a purposeful and fulfilling life beyond her recovery. Her battle with addiction was a turbulent chapter that tested her strength, eroded her self-esteem, and disconnected her from the joys of everyday life. Yet, it also laid the groundwork for a profound transformation marked by self-discovery, resilience, and a renewed sense of direction.

The turning point for Emily came when she embraced recovery, a decision that, while lifesaving, introduced her to a new set of challenges. Sobriety brought clarity but also forced her to confront the void that her addiction had masked. The question of "What now?" loomed large, prompting Emily to seek meaning that would redefine her existence.

Emily's search began with reconnecting with herself, a process that involved peeling back the layers of her addiction to rediscover the interests, passions, and values that her struggles had obscured. She revisited old hobbies and explored new activities, from painting and writing to hiking and meditation. Each activity was a step towards understanding herself better and healing the wounds of her past.

However, Emily's quest for purpose extended beyond personal fulfillment. She recognized that her journey through addiction and recovery had equipped her with unique insights and empathy that could be invaluable to others facing similar battles. This realization sparked a desire to give back, transforming her pursuit of purpose into a mission to help others.

Emily began volunteering at local recovery centres, sharing her story and supporting those recovering. Her message was one of hope and solidarity, a reminder that while the path to sobriety is fraught with challenges, it is also ripe with the possibility of reinvention and growth.

Her involvement with the recovery community deepened her understanding of the systemic issues surrounding addiction and recovery, fueling her passion for advocacy. Emily became involved in initiatives aimed at destigmatizing addiction and improving access to recovery resources, leveraging her personal experience to champion change at a broader level.

As Emily's journey unfolded, she found that her quest for purpose was not a destination but a continually evolving path. Each step forward revealed new avenues for growth and contribution, from pursuing formal education in counseling to starting a blog where she shared her experiences and insights about recovery, mental health, and finding purpose after addiction.

Through her quest, Emily discovered that fulfillment lay not in the absence of challenges but in pursuing a life aligned with her values and passions. Her story is a testament to the power of resilience and the transformative potential of seeking purpose in the aftermath of adversity. It underscores the idea that recovery from addiction is not just about overcoming a dependence on substances but about rebuilding a life filled with meaning, connection, and joy.

Today, Emily's life is a vibrant tapestry of personal achievements, community engagement, and advocacy work, each element reflecting her commitment to living purposefully. Her journey from addiction to a life of fulfillment and service is a source of inspiration, demonstrating that it is possible to emerge from the shadow of past mistakes to create a future defined by hope, purpose, and the endless capacity for renewal.

# CHAPTER 6

## THE HEALING POWER OF CREATIVITY

In the mosaic of human experience, creativity emerges as a powerful force for healing, transformation, and self-discovery. Creative healing refers to the process of engaging in artistic and creative activities as a means to foster emotional well-being, cope with trauma, and navigate the complexities of mental health challenges. It's a journey that transcends traditional forms of expression, tapping into the innate capacity for resilience and growth within each of us. This introduction explores the essence of creative healing, its benefits, and how it serves as a beacon of light for those seeking solace and understanding amid life's storms.

At its core, creative healing is about using art, music, writing, dance, and other creative outlets as tools for communication and self-exploration. It operates on the premise that a profound connection exists between the act of creation and the healing process. Through creative expression, individuals are given a voice when words fall short, a means to externalize feelings, thoughts, and experiences that are otherwise difficult to articulate. It's a form of language that speaks in colors, shapes, rhythms, and narratives, bridging the gap between the inner and outer worlds.

The potential of creativity to promote reflection and self-awareness is what gives it its therapeutic value. Engaging in creative activities encourages individuals to delve into their subconscious, unveiling hidden emotions, uncovering past traumas, and confronting unresolved conflicts. This process of self-discovery can be both enlightening and cathartic, offering insights into personal struggles and facilitating a deeper understanding of one. It's an introspective journey and reflective practice that can result in significant personal development and increased clarity.

Moreover, creative healing provides a safe space for emotional expression and release. Creating can be immensely liberating, allowing individuals to channel their emotions into their work, transforming pain and suffering into something tangible and often beautiful. This emotional release can be therapeutic, reducing stress, alleviating anxiety, and diminishing symptoms of depression. It's a way of coping that doesn't just help to manage difficult emotions but also transforms the healing process into an empowering experience of self-expression and resilience.

Creative healing also fosters a sense of connection and belonging. Artistic endeavors often unite people through collaborative projects, workshops, or sharing sessions. These communal experiences can help to alleviate feelings of isolation, build supportive networks, and cultivate empathy by sharing stories and experiences. This way, creative healing extends beyond the individual, nurturing a sense of community and shared humanity.

The benefits of creative healing are not limited to those with a background in art or those who consider themselves "creative." It is accessible to everyone, regardless of artistic skill or experience. The focus is not on the outcome or aesthetic value of the creation but on the process itself and its personal meaning. This inclusivity is one of the strengths of creative healing, emphasizing the universal capacity for creativity and its role in emotional and psychological well-being.

Incorporating creative healing into one's life doesn't require grand gestures or elaborate projects. It may be as easy as penning a poem, dancing to your favorite music, playing an instrument, or scribbling in a notepad. The key is to engage in these activities with an open heart and mind, allowing them to be vehicles for exploration, expression, and healing.

Creative healing is a monument to the human spirit's tenacity and the transforming potential of art as we traverse life's obstacles. It is a reminder that within each of us lies a wellspring of creativity, ready to be tapped into as a source of strength, healing, and renewal. Through creative healing, we learn not only to cope with the vicissitudes of life but also to thrive, finding beauty and meaning amid adversity. It is a journey that reaffirms the power of creativity to heal, transform, and illuminate the path to wholeness and well-being.

## Art Therapy Basics

Art therapy is a profound bridge between the visual arts and the healing journey, offering a non-verbal language through which individuals can express their thoughts, feelings, and experiences. It merges the creative process with psychological therapy, providing a unique avenue for personal growth, insight, and healing. Art therapy is based on the belief that creating art can be therapeutic and transformative. Here, we delve into the basics of art therapy, its principles, processes, and its impact on individuals seeking healing and understanding.

### Foundations of Art Therapy

Art therapy rests on the foundational principle that creative expression can foster mental and emotional well-being. It is run by a licensed art therapist who guides the process, assisting people in exploring and resolving emotional conflicts, developing self-awareness, managing behavior and addictions, improving reality orientation, fostering social skills, lowering anxiety, and boosting self-esteem.

**The Therapeutic Process**

The process of art therapy is not about creating aesthetically pleasing artwork but about the expression of one's inner world. Participants are encouraged to create art that reflects their feelings, thoughts, and experiences. This can include drawing, painting, sculpting, collage, and other forms of visual art. The therapist may provide prompts or themes to explore, or the participant may choose what they wish to express.

Through the act of creation, individuals can uncover and explore underlying thoughts and feelings that may be difficult to articulate verbally. The art becomes a medium for communication, a way to say what words cannot. After the creation process, the therapist and the individual may discuss the artwork, exploring its meanings, themes, and what it reveals about the individual's emotional state or experiences. This reflective process can lead to pivotal insights and understanding for healing.

**Benefits of Art Therapy**

Art therapy offers many benefits for individuals across all age groups and backgrounds. It offers a secure and encouraging setting where people may examine their emotions, ideas, and actions. Some of the key benefits include:

Emotional Release: For those coping with stress, trauma, or emotional issues, art therapy offers a cathartic means of expressing and releasing feelings.

Self-Discovery: Through the creative process, individuals can explore different aspects of their personalities and experiences, leading to greater self-awareness and insight.

Stress Reduction: Making art may be a contemplative practice that lowers tension and encourages serenity and relaxation.

Improved Self-Esteem: When a work of art is finished, one feels accomplished and their confidence and self-worth increase.

Enhanced Communication Skills: People can learn how to express their thoughts and feelings more effectively via art therapy, which can help them communicate more effectively.

**Application and Accessibility**

One of the most appealing aspects of art therapy is its versatility and accessibility. People coping with a variety of psychological conditions, including as trauma, depression, anxiety, addiction, and chronic disease, may find it helpful. Art therapy can be practiced in various settings, including hospitals, rehabilitation centers, schools, community centers, and private practices.

In addition, anyone may benefit from art therapy without having to be an artist. It's an inclusive practice that welcomes individuals at all levels of artistic experience. The focus is on the creation process and the therapeutic benefits of self-expression, not on the technical skills or the final product.

Art therapy stands as a testament to the healing power of creativity. It underscores the connection between artistic expression and psychological well-being, offering a unique and powerful tool for personal growth, healing, and transformation. Through art therapy, individuals can navigate the complexities of their emotions and experiences, finding clarity, comfort, and a deeper understanding of themselves.

## Writing for Wellness

Writing for wellness encapsulates the transformative power of words to heal, explore, and express our innermost thoughts and feelings. It's a practice rooted in the understanding that writing can be a therapeutic tool, offering a safe and accessible means to confront emotions, experiences, and memories. This approach to writing goes beyond mere documentation, serving as a bridge to greater self-awareness, emotional release, and psychological well-being.

**The Therapeutic Power of Writing**

Writing for wellness leverages writing as a form of therapy, inviting individuals to express themselves freely and without judgment. This practice can take many forms, including journaling, poetry, storytelling, and letter writing. Each form offers a unique pathway to exploring one's internal world, providing a means to articulate what may be difficult to say out loud.

**Benefits of Writing for Wellness**

The benefits of writing for wellness are manifold, touching on various aspects of mental and emotional health:

**Emotional Release:** Writing provides an outlet for expressing emotions, allowing for the articulation of joy, sorrow, frustration, and hope. This act of expression can be a powerful cathartic experience, helping to alleviate emotional burden and stress.

**Clarifying Thoughts and Feelings**: Writing encourages reflection and introspection, aiding individuals in organizing their thoughts and emotions. This clarity can lead to greater understanding and insight into one's mental and emotional states.

**Problem Solving:** Writing about challenges or conflicts can help in identifying solutions. Putting problems into words can make them more manageable and open new perspectives for resolving issues.

**Enhancing Self-Reflection and Growth:** Regular writing encourages a deeper exploration of personal experiences and beliefs, fostering self-discovery and personal growth. It's a way to track progress, recognize patterns, and set goals for the future.

**Reducing Stress and Anxiety:** Engaging in writing can have a meditative effect, focusing the mind and providing a break from negative thought cycles. This can help people feel calmer and more relaxed by lowering their stress and anxiety levels.

### How to Incorporate Writing into Your Wellness Routine

Incorporating writing into your wellness routine doesn't require specialized skills or a significant time commitment. Here are some ways to get started:

**Journaling:** Daily or weekly journal expressing your thoughts, feelings, and experiences. This can be a private space for self-reflection or a creative outlet for storytelling.

**Gratitude Writing**: Dedicate time to write about things you're grateful for. This practice can shift focus from lacking to the abundance present in your life, fostering positivity.

**Letter Writing:** Write letters to yourself, loved ones, or even people with whom you have unresolved issues (these don't need to be sent). This can be a way to express unspoken feelings or to offer forgiveness.

**Mindful Writing:** Compose concentrating on the here and now, writing with all of your might. Present-moment awareness and mindfulness may be improved by doing this.

**Creative Writing:** Experiment with poetry, short stories, or other creative writing forms to explore your imagination and express yourself in new and inventive ways.

## Writing for Wellness in Practice

The key to writing for wellness is consistency and honesty. It's about creating a habit that feels supportive and enriching. Approach writing with an open heart and mind, allowing yourself to explore the depths of your experiences without censorship. Remember, the goal is not to produce polished writing pieces but to engage in the process as a means of healing and self-discovery.

Writing for wellness is a journey of exploration, a dialogue between the pen and the soul. It's a practice that embraces the messy, beautiful, and complex tapestry of human experience, offering a path to more excellent emotional and psychological health. Through writing, we may discover resilience, find serenity, and skillfully and compassionately traverse the complexities of our inner worlds.

## Music as Medicine

Often hailed as the universal language, music transcends mere entertainment to serve as a potent tool for healing and emotional expression. The concept of music as medicine is ancient, yet it continues to be validated by modern science, revealing its profound impact on the human psyche and body. This exploration into music's therapeutic potential unveils how melodies, harmonies, and rhythms can comfort the soul, mend the heart, and rejuvenate the spirit.

## The Healing Power of Music

Music's ability to heal and soothe is multifaceted. It influences our emotions, physiological responses, and cognitive processes. It can elevate mood, reduce anxiety, alleviate pain, and even improve sleep quality. Using music to meet people's physical, emotional, cognitive, and social needs, music therapy is a well-established health profession that takes use of these advantages.

## Emotional Expression and Release

Music offers a unique avenue for emotional expression and catharsis. Certain songs can resonate with our feelings, helping to articulate emotions we might struggle to express otherwise. For someone grappling with grief, listening to a sad melody can provide solace, validating their sorrow and offering a sense of shared experience. Conversely, an upbeat tune can uplift spirits, encouraging movement and joy even in challenging times.

### Physiological Impact

The physiological effects of music are profound and wide-ranging. According to research, listening to music can lower cortisol levels—a hormone linked to stress—as well as blood pressure and heart rate. For patients undergoing surgery or those in recovery, music has been shown to reduce perceived pain levels and anxiety, contributing to a quicker and more comfortable healing process.

### Cognitive Benefits

Music also holds significant cognitive benefits, particularly in memory recall and mental performance. For individuals with Alzheimer's or dementia, familiar music can unlock memories and emotions, offering moments of clarity and connection. Additionally, music can enhance focus and productivity, making it a valuable tool for learning and concentration.

### Social Connection

Music fosters social cohesion, bridging individuals across cultures and experiences. Group musical activities, like choirs or drum circles, promote a sense of belonging and community. These interactions can be incredibly healing, providing a supportive environment where individuals can share joy, creativity, and mutual support.

## Incorporating Music into Healing Practices

Adopting music as a component of your wellness routine can be simple and profoundly impactful. Here are some ways to harness the healing power of music:

**Personalized Playlists:** Create playlists that resonate with moods or needs, such as relaxation, motivation, or comfort. Listening to music that aligns with your emotional state can be incredibly therapeutic.

**Active Listening:** Set aside time for active listening, where you fully immerse yourself in the music. Pay attention to the lyrics, melodies, and instruments, allowing yourself to feel the emotions the piece conveys.

**Music Making:** Engaging in music-making, whether playing an instrument, singing, or composing, can be a powerful form of self-expression and emotional release.

**Therapeutic Music Programs**: Consider participating in music therapy sessions or therapeutic music programs. Trained professionals guide these and can be tailored to address specific therapeutic goals.

**Meditative Music:** Incorporate music into meditation or relaxation routines. Certain types of music, especially those with slow tempos and smooth melodies, can enhance the contemplative experience, fostering deep relaxation and mindfulness.

Music as medicine is a testament to the art form's profound impact on human health and well-being. It underscores the intricate connection between the arts and healing, inviting us to explore music's potential as a source of enjoyment and a companion on our journey toward wellness and recovery. Through the universal language of music, we can find comfort, expression, and connection, tapping into its timeless power to heal the body and the soul.

## Crafting and DIY Projects

Crafting and do-it-yourself (DIY) projects are more than just hobbies; they're pathways to healing and personal fulfillment. Immersing oneself in the creation of something tangible engages the mind, hands, and heart, offering a unique blend of concentration, creativity, and catharsis. This process of making, whether through knitting, woodworking, painting, or any other form of crafting, stands as a testament to the human desire to create and find solace in the act of creation.

The therapeutic value of crafting lies in its ability to anchor us in the present moment, focusing our thoughts on the task at hand and allowing us to step away from the whirlwind of daily stresses and worries. It's a form of mindfulness that brings a sense of calm and centeredness, much needed in today's fast-paced world. Each stitch in a knitting project, stroke of paint on canvas, or cut in a piece of wood is a step away from chaos and towards inner peace.

Moreover, crafting and DIY projects offer tangible achievement and self-efficacy. Finishing a project, no matter how small, can boost self-esteem and provide a feeling of accomplishment that's often hard to come by in the more intangible areas of our lives. This sense of progress and completion is significant for individuals who may feel stuck or overwhelmed by life's challenges. It's a reminder that they can set goals and see them through, a valuable lesson that can be applied to more significant life situations.

Crafting also opens avenues for personal expression and creativity that may be stifled in other areas of life. It allows for experimentation, risk-taking, and innovation, providing a safe space to explore new ideas and aspects of oneself. This freedom to create without judgment or external pressures can lead to profound self-discovery and growth. Through crafting, individuals can communicate their identity, experiences, and emotions in a way that words cannot fully capture.

Participating in crafts and do-it-yourself projects can help strengthen ties to the community. Many crafters enjoy sharing their projects, techniques, and experiences with others, whether in person through workshops and crafting circles or online through forums and social media. This sharing of knowledge and skills builds a supportive network that celebrates creativity and collaboration, offering a sense of belonging and mutual respect among like-minded individuals.

Additionally, crafting has the unique ability to bridge generations, cultures, and backgrounds. It's a way to preserve traditional skills and knowledge, passing them down through families and communities. For many, crafting is a link to their heritage, a way to keep traditions alive and connect with their ancestors. It's also a celebration of cultural diversity, with different crafts offering a glimpse into various communities' customs, values, and aesthetics worldwide.

Incorporating crafting and DIY projects into one's life doesn't require expertise or expensive materials. It starts with a simple desire to create and the willingness to embrace the process, regardless of the outcome. The key is to find joy in the act of making, to celebrate the small victories, and to learn from the mishaps. Whether it's repurposing old items, creating handmade gifts, or simply experimenting with new materials and techniques, crafting is a journey that rewards patience, creativity, and perseverance.

Crafting and DIY projects embody the transformative power of making. They provide a comprehensive method of treatment that takes social, emotional, and mental health into account. Through crafting, individuals can find purpose, express their creativity, and connect with a community of makers. It's a celebration of the human capacity to create beauty from raw materials, to transform ideas into reality, and to find healing and fulfillment in the process.

# CHAPTER 7

## REBUILDING RELATIONSHIPS

Rebuilding relationships after the transformative experiences of incarceration or addiction involves navigating a landscape filled with both challenges and opportunities for growth. Trust, once fractured, requires time, patience, and genuine effort to mend. This journey is about restoring what was lost and forging deeper connections through improved communication, empathy, and a renewed commitment to mutual understanding and respect. It requires striking a careful balance between taking care of oneself and the people we love, all the while setting up sound limits that provide a secure and encouraging atmosphere for everyone.

Reconnecting with loved ones can be daunting. The fear of judgment, rejection, or misunderstanding looms large, creating open and honest communication barriers. Yet, true healing and reconnection can begin through facing these fears and stepping into vulnerable spaces. Learning to express oneself clearly and listen actively becomes paramount, as does the ability to articulate needs and expectations in a way that honors both oneself and the other person.

Equally important is the journey of understanding and compassion—recognizing that the effects of incarceration or addiction extend beyond the individual to touch the lives of friends, family members, and partners. These relationships may have been tested, strained, or altered by the experience, requiring all parties to navigate the complexities of emotions such as hurt, anger, and disappointment.

Setting healthy boundaries is another critical aspect of rebuilding relationships. These boundaries are not barriers to keep people out but guidelines that help ensure interactions are respectful, nurturing, and conducive to growth. They protect the well-being of everyone involved, enabling individuals to support each other without compromising their mental health or recovery process.

In the end, the process of mending a relationship is proof of the human spirit's tenacity and the strength of love and forgiveness. It's a path marked by moments of vulnerability, strength, and profound transformation, offering the promise of renewed connections that are stronger and more meaningful than ever before.

## Activities: Reflective Journaling

Reflective journaling, mainly through writing letters to oneself or a loved one, stands as a powerful tool in the journey of rebuilding relationships after significant life challenges such as incarceration or overcoming addiction. This activity invites deep introspection and honest expression, critical components in healing and understanding.

Objective: To foster self-awareness, enhance communication, and facilitate emotional healing within relationships.

Materials Needed: Pen and paper or a digital writing tool.

**Instructions**

**1. Set Aside Dedicated Time:** Pick a calm, cozy area where you can think clearly without being disturbed. Make time to really interact with your ideas and emotions.

**2. Reflect on the Relationship**: Think back on the course of your relationship, its highs and lows. Think back on the difficulties you've encountered, the development you've gone through, and the adjustments you wish to see. All of your feelings, including gratitude, remorse, hope, and forgiveness, should be acknowledged and processed.

**3. Writing the Letter:** Begin your letter by addressing yourself or your loved one in a compassionate and open-hearted manner. There's no right or wrong way to do this; let your thoughts flow naturally. You might want to cover the following points:

- Your feelings about the current state of the relationship.
- Significant challenges you've faced together and individually.
- Personal growth and changes you've noticed in yourself and your loved one.
- Your hopes and intentions for the future of the relationship.
- Expressions of gratitude, forgiveness, or understanding that you wish to convey.

**4. Review and Reflect:** Once you've finished writing, take some time to review what you've written. Reflect on the process of writing the letter itself—how it made you feel, any insights you gained, and whether it shifted your perspective on the relationship.

**5. Decide on Sharing:** Consider whether you'd like to share the letter with the person it's addressed to. Sharing can be a decisive step toward rebuilding trust and understanding but ensure you're ready and it feels appropriate. If the letter is to yourself, keep it in a safe place where you can revisit it in the future.

**6. Follow-Up Conversation**: If you choose to share your letter, having a follow-up conversation about the contents might be helpful. This can be an opportunity to discuss feelings, clarify intentions, and make plans for moving forward together.

**Benefits**

- Enhances emotional clarity and self-awareness.
- Promotes healing and understanding within the relationship.
- Encourages open and honest communication.
- Serves as a tangible reminder of personal and relational growth.

Reflective journaling through letter writing is more than just an exercise; it's a bridge to deeper connection and mutual understanding. It's about uncovering the heart of the relationship, facing its complexities with courage, and committing to a path of growth and healing together.

## Activities: Communication Role-Play

Engaging in communication role-play with a trusted friend or mentor is a dynamic and effective way to enhance your communication skills, particularly in the context of rebuilding relationships after significant life events like incarceration or addiction recovery. Through the simulation of real-life encounters, this exercise offers a secure and supportive setting to practice expressing your needs, actively listening, and reacting with empathy.

**Objective:** To improve communication skills, including expressing needs clearly, listening actively, and responding empathetically.

**Materials Needed:** None.

**Instructions**

**1. Choose a Partner:** Select a trusted friend, family member, or mentor willing to participate in the role-play. It's essential that this person understands the purpose of the activity and is committed to supporting your growth.

**2. Set the Scene:** Together, decide on a few scenarios that reflect common communication challenges within your relationships. These could include discussing a sensitive topic, asking for support, or addressing a misunderstanding. Try to choose situations relevant to your experiences and offer potential for growth.

**3. Assign Roles:** For each scenario, assign roles between you and your partner. One person will play 'themselves' in the scenario context, while the other adopts the role of the person you're practicing communicating with. Switch roles as needed to gain perspective from both sides.

**4. Role-Play the Scenario:** Begin the role-play, focusing on the objectives of expressing needs, listening actively, and responding with empathy. The person in their role should practice articulating their thoughts and feelings clearly and respectfully. The person in the other role should focus on listening without interrupting, acknowledging the other's perspective, and responding to demonstrate understanding and empathy.

**5. Reflect and Discuss:** Reflect on the interaction after each scenario. Discuss what felt challenging, what strategies were effective, and how the experience could be applied to real-life situations. This reflection is crucial for turning the role-play experience into actionable insights.

**6. Provide Feedback:** Offer each other constructive feedback, highlighting strengths in communication and areas for improvement. Feedback should be specific, actionable, and delivered with kindness.

**7. Repeat:** If desired, repeat the activity with different scenarios to continue building your communication skills. Each role-play aims to incorporate feedback and new strategies to enhance the interaction.

**Benefits**

- Enhances ability to express needs and feelings clearly and respectfully.
- Improves active listening skills, including giving full attention and demonstrating understanding.
- Fosters empathetic responses that validate the other person's perspective.
- Builds confidence in handling difficult conversations and strengthens overall communication skills.

Communication role-play is not just about practicing what to say but also about understanding how to say it and how to listen. It's a holistic approach to communication that acknowledges the complexity of human interactions and the importance of empathy and respect. By engaging in this activity, you're taking a proactive step towards rebuilding and strengthening your relationships, equipped with the skills to navigate conversations with greater understanding and compassion.

## Activities: Gratitude List

Creating a gratitude list focused on the positive aspects and moments within your relationships is an uplifting and transformative activity that can significantly enhance their dynamics. This exercise encourages you to shift focus from challenges and conflicts to appreciation and thankfulness, fostering a more positive and supportive environment for connection and growth.

**Objective:** To identify and appreciate the positive aspects and moments of gratitude in your relationships and understand how this practice can positively affect your relationship dynamics.

**Materials Needed:** Notebook or digital document, pen or keyboard.

**Instructions**

**1. Choose a Quiet Time and Space**: Find a comfortable and quiet space to reflect without distractions. Set aside uninterrupted time for this activity so you can genuinely engage with the process.

**2. Reflect on Your Relationships:** Think about the critical relationships you wish to focus on. These could be with family members, friends, partners, or colleagues. Bring each person to mind and consider your relationship with them.

**3. Start Your Gratitude List:** List specific things you are grateful for in each relationship. These can include:

Personal qualities of the individual that you admire or appreciate (e.g., their kindness, sense of humor, supportiveness).

- Positive experiences or memories you've shared.
- Acts of kindness or support they've provided.
- Ways in which they've inspired or encouraged you.

Anything else that comes to mind sparks gratitude when you think of them?

**4. Reflect on the Impact:** After you've compiled your list, take some time to reflect on how recognizing these positive aspects makes you feel about each relationship. Think about the future dynamics of your relationships and how this change in emphasis may affect them.

**5. Share Your Gratitude (Optional)**: If you feel comfortable, consider sharing your gratitude with the people you've written about. This can be done verbally, through a letter, or any other communication you prefer. Sharing your appreciation can strengthen bonds and bring new openness and positivity to your relationships.

**6. Make It a Regular Practice:** Gratitude is most effective when practiced regularly. Consider making your gratitude list a weekly or monthly practice to cultivate a positive perspective on your relationships.

**Benefits:**

- It enhances positive emotions and reduces the tendency to focus on negatives within relationships.
- Strengthens bonds by openly acknowledging and appreciating the value of others in your life.
- Encourages a culture of appreciation and kindness within your relationships.

It improves overall relationship satisfaction by focusing on the good and fostering a more supportive and loving environment.

Making a thankfulness list is an easy, but effective, method to change the way you think about your relationships. You may improve your mental health and foster a more positive, appreciative, and helpful dynamic in your relationships by consciously recognizing and appreciating the good things in life and the moments when you are grateful. This practice serves as a reminder of the good within our connections with others, even amidst challenges, and highlights the importance of gratitude in nurturing and sustaining healthy, fulfilling relationships.

## Activities: Boundary-Setting Exercise

Healthy personal boundaries are essential for maintaining well-being and fostering respectful, fulfilling relationships. Establishing boundaries enables us to specify our comfort zones and ideal treatment standards from others. This activity focuses on identifying your boundaries, practicing articulating them clearly, and discussing strategies to enforce them respectfully.

**Objective:** To identify personal boundaries crucial for your well-being and develop skills for articulating and enforcing these boundaries respectfully.

**Materials Needed:** A notebook or digital document for reflection and planning, pen or keyboard.

**Instructions**

**1. Reflect on Your Needs and Limits**: Reflect on past experiences in your relationships. Consider situations where you felt uncomfortable, disrespected, or drained. What boundaries, if they had been in place, could have prevented these feelings? Consider your values, principles, and what you need to feel respected, safe, and comfortable in your interactions.

**2. Identify Your Boundaries:** Based on your reflection, identify specific boundaries essential to your well-being. These relate to your emotional, physical, time or energy limits. Examples could include needing personal space, limits on how others speak to you, or how much of your time and resources you can commit to others. Write these down clearly and concisely.

**3. Practice Articulating Your Boundaries**: Once you have identified your boundaries, practice articulating them. It's essential to communicate your boundaries clearly, assertively, and respectfully. You might say, "I value our time together, but I need some time alone to recharge. Can we plan our meetings so I can have some quiet time afterward?" or "I feel disrespected when raised voices are used in a conversation. Can we agree to discuss things calmly?"

**4. Role-Playing for Confidence:** Practice role-playing with a trusted friend or family member where you articulate your boundaries. This can help build confidence in expressing your boundaries in real-life situations. Ask for feedback on your delivery and whether your message was clear and respectful.

**5. Discuss Enforcement Strategies:** Reflect on and discuss (with your practice partner, if using one) strategies for enforcing your boundaries if they are not respected. This could include removing yourself from a situation, reiterating your boundary in a firmer tone, or seeking external support in cases where boundaries are repeatedly ignored.

**6. Commit to Respectful Enforcement**: Commit yourself to enforce your boundaries respectfully. Recall that establishing boundaries is about taking ownership of your Well-being and the treatment you accept from others, not about exerting control over others.

**7. Regular Review and Adjustment**: Recognize that your needs and, consequently, your boundaries may change over time. Establish a routine of periodically reviewing and modifying your limits as necessary to make sure they continue to successfully support your well-being.

**Benefits**

- It enhances self-respect and encourages others to treat you with respect.
- Reduces feelings of resentment and discomfort by preventing overextension and disrespect.

- Improves communication and deepens trust in relationships.

Fosters autonomy and empowerment by taking charge of your personal space and needs.

Identifying and articulating personal boundaries are crucial for self-care and healthy relationship dynamics. Through this exercise, you become more aware of your needs and limits and gain the confidence to communicate and enforce these boundaries, thereby promoting a culture of mutual respect and understanding in your interactions with others.

## Activities: Trust-Building Plan

Rebuilding trust in a relationship is a deliberate and sensitive process that requires commitment, patience, and clear communication from all involved parties. Trust, once broken, can often feel like a shattered vase—while it can be put back together, the cracks might still show. However, with care, understanding, and dedication, these cracks can become symbols of resilience and growth. Developing a trust-building plan is about setting actionable steps, timelines, and goals to mend the relationship and nurture trust once again.

**Objective:** To create a structured plan for rebuilding trust in a key relationship, outlining specific actions, timelines, and mutual goals.

**Materials Needed:** Writing tools (pen and paper, digital document), a calm and open mindset.

**Instructions**

**1. Open Dialogue:** Start with an open and honest conversation about the desire to rebuild trust. Acknowledge past hurts and express a mutual commitment to healing and moving forward.

This conversation sets the foundation for your trust-building plan.

**2. Identify Key Issues:** Identify the core issues that led to the erosion of trust. Be specific about incidents, behaviors, or patterns that must be addressed. This step requires vulnerability and honesty from both parties.

**3. Set Clear Goals**: Define what a successful rebuilding of trust looks like for each person. Objectives have to be time-bound, relevant, measurable, attainable, and specified (SMART). For example, "Within three months, we will establish a weekly check-in to openly discuss our feelings and progress."

**4. Outline Specific Actions:** Break down your goals into actionable steps. If communication was an issue, one action might be to attend a communication skills workshop together. If commitment was the issue, an action could be planning future activities demonstrating dedication to the relationship.

**5. Establish Timelines:** Assign realistic timelines to each action step. Timelines help keep the process on track and provide milestones to celebrate progress.

**6. Agree on Accountability Measures**: Decide how you will hold each other accountable for taking the agreed-upon actions. This might involve regular check-ins or working with a relationship counselor.

**7. Implement and Adjust:** Start implementing your plan, staying flexible and open to adjustments. Rebuilding trust is a dynamic process that may require changes as you learn and grow together.

**8. Celebrate Progress**: No matter how tiny, acknowledge and appreciate your accomplishments. Acknowledging accomplishments and efforts is essential to sustaining motivation and bolstering confidence.

**9. Regular Review:** Set dates for reviewing your trust-building plan. Discuss what's working, what isn't, and how you can further adjust your actions and goals to continue moving forward.

**Benefits**

- Creates a shared understanding of the issues at hand and a mutual commitment to resolving them.
- Provides a clear roadmap for healing, reducing feelings of overwhelm by breaking the process into manageable steps.
- Encourages accountability and transparency, which are foundational for trust.
- Reinforces progress, helping both parties see and appreciate the work done to mend the relationship.

This trust-building plan is a structured approach to navigating the complexities of healing a relationship. It acknowledges that restoring trust is a process that calls for patience, diligence, and dedication. By outlining specific actions, timelines, and goals, the plan offers a tangible framework for this journey, promoting a sense of shared responsibility and progress. Through this process, trust can be rebuilt, making the relationship more substantial and more resilient than before.

## Activities: Empathy Mapping

Empathy mapping is an imaginative and perceptive exercise that explores the thoughts, emotions, and experiences of others to help you better understand and connect with them. It's a tool that fosters empathy, enabling you to see the world through another's eyes, feel what they feel, and understand their thoughts and motivations. This exercise can be precious in relationships where rebuilding trust, enhancing communication, and fostering deeper connections are goals.

**Objective:** To create a visual representation (map) of another person's perspective to enhance understanding and empathy in relationships.

**Materials Needed**: Large paper or digital drawing tool, markers or drawing software, and an open, curious mindset.

**Instructions**

**Choose a Relationship Focus:** Select a relationship you wish to explore and enhance through this activity. It could be with a family member, friend, partner, or colleague.

**Prepare Your Empathy Map Canvas:**

- Draw a large square on your paper or digital canvas.
- Divide it into four quadrants.
- Label them as follows: Says, Thinks, Does, and Feels.

**Gather Insights:**

In the Says quadrant, jot down things the person often says in conversations. What words do they use? What topics do they talk about?

In the Thinks quadrant, reflect on what you believe this person thinks about but might not say out loud. What concerns or dreams do they have?

The Does quadrant is for actions. What actions do they take that provide insight into their feelings or thoughts?

In the Feels quadrant, try to empathize with their feelings based on their words, thoughts, and actions. This requires you to infer emotions they might not have explicitly expressed.

**Reflect and Analyze:** Once you've filled out each quadrant, look back at the map. What new insights do you gain about this person's perspective and the emotional world? How do their feelings, thoughts, actions, and words interconnect?

**Develop Actionable Insights:** Based on your empathy map, identify ways to improve your interactions with this person. Are there specific needs or emotions you can address? How can you adjust your communication or behavior to foster a more profound connection?

**Share and Discuss (Optional):** If appropriate, and you feel it would be beneficial, share your empathy map with the person it's about. Use it as a starting point for a deeper conversation about your relationship, perspectives, and how you can better support each other.

**Benefits**

- Promotes a deeper understanding of another's perspective, enhancing empathy and connection.
- It helps identify misunderstandings or gaps in communication that can be addressed.
- Encourages a more thoughtful and compassionate approach to interactions.
- It can reveal underlying emotions or thoughts that influence relationship dynamics, offering opportunities for growth and improvement.

Empathy mapping is a powerful exercise in building emotional intelligence and fostering connections. By taking the time to consider the thoughts, feelings, actions, and words of others, we open ourselves up to a deeper level of understanding and compassion. This tool enhances our relationships and enriches our emotional lives, teaching us the value of looking beyond the surface to the rich, emotional world beneath.

# CHAPTER 8

## NURTURING PHYSICAL HEALTH AS A FOUNDATION FOR MENTAL WELL-BEING

Nurturing physical health is an essential pillar in the foundation of mental well-being. The intricate connection between the body and mind underscores the importance of physical care in maintaining and enhancing psychological health. This symbiotic relationship means that when we take steps to care for our bodies, we simultaneously support our mental and emotional landscapes. This chapter delves into how physical health impacts our mental state and provides practical advice on incorporating physical wellness into our daily lives. By understanding and applying these principles, we can create a balanced approach to health that honors and nurtures our physical and mental well-being, setting the stage for a more fulfilled and harmonious life.

## Exercise and Recovery

Exercise is not just a cornerstone of physical health; it's a powerful catalyst for mental and emotional recovery. Integrating exercise into one's lifestyle can profoundly impact the journey toward healing from various forms of mental distress, including the aftermath of addiction, depression, anxiety, and other mental health challenges. The role of recovery exercise is multifaceted, offering benefits far beyond the physical realm.

### The Psychological Benefits of Exercise

**Boosts Mood:** Exercise improves your well-being by releasing endorphins and other naturally occurring brain chemicals. This biochemical process can produce feelings of happiness and euphoria, often referred to as the "runner's high," providing a natural counter to depression and negativity.

**Reduces Stress:** Exercise is a potent stress reliever. Increased norepinephrine concentrations result from physical exercise, and this hormone can help modulate the brain's reaction to stress. It also promotes relaxation and dissipates tension in the body and mind, assisting individuals to cope with stress more effectively.

**Improves Sleep:** Regular physical activity can help normalize sleep patterns often disrupted by mental health issues or recovery processes. By promoting physical fatigue, exercise encourages more profound and restorative sleep, essential for mental health and recovery.

**Enhances Self-Esteem:** Consistent exercise improves physical appearance and capabilities, significantly boosting self-esteem and confidence. Reaching any size of fitness objective may bring one a sense of success that balances out the worthlessness or powerlessness that are frequently connected to mental health issues.

**Fosters Social Interaction:** Exercise programs, fitness classes, and sports provide positive opportunities for social interaction that can reduce feelings of isolation and loneliness. The sense of support and belonging that these group activities offer is essential to the rehabilitation of mental health.

### Exercise as a Tool for Recovery

In the context of recovery, especially from mental health conditions or addiction, exercise takes on a deeper meaning than simple physical activity. It becomes a systematic approach toward reconstructing one's life. It introduces routine and discipline, critical elements often lost in the throes of mental health challenges. A regular exercise schedule can impart a sense of normalcy and control, providing a constructive focus and a break from the mental and emotional turmoil.

**Cognitive Clarity:** It has been demonstrated that physical exercise enhances cognitive abilities such as memory, focus, and processing speed. This cognitive clarity is particularly beneficial in recovery, aiding individuals in therapy, counseling, and other mental health treatments by enhancing their ability to absorb and apply therapeutic concepts and strategies.

**Emotional Regulation:** Exercise can act as a natural form of emotion regulation, offering an outlet for frustration, anger, and tension. Physical exertion allows for expressing and releasing these emotions in a healthy, controlled environment, promoting emotional stability.

**Building Resilience:** The challenges faced during exercise, such as pushing through physical discomfort or overcoming performance plateaus, can translate into increased psychological resilience. The determination and perseverance developed through regular physical activity equip individuals with the mental fortitude to face and overcome the obstacles inherent in the recovery process.

### Integrating Exercise into Recovery

Incorporating exercise into the recovery journey requires a mindful approach that respects the individual's physical and mental conditions. It's not about intensity or performance but finding enjoyable, feasible, and sustainable activities. This could mean starting with gentle activities like walking, yoga, or swimming and gradually increasing intensity as confidence and physical fitness improve. The secret is to be consistent and include exercise in your daily schedule.

Recognizing that the advantages of exercise build up gradually, it's also critical to set reasonable objectives and acknowledge accomplishments. Patience and perseverance are essential, as is listening to one's body and adjusting activities to avoid burnout or injury.

Exercise embodies a powerful healing force capable of transforming the body, mind, and spirit. Its role in recovery extends far beyond the physical, touching on the emotional, psychological, and social aspects of healing. By embracing exercise as a regular part of life, individuals on the path to recovery can harness its benefits to support their journey towards mental well-being, strength, clarity, and joy in the movement towards a healthier, more balanced life.

## Nutrition's Role in Mental Health

A topic of growing attention and significance in health and well-being is the complex tango between diet and mental health. What we consume doesn't just fuel our bodies; it profoundly impacts our mental and emotional states. Nutrition's role in mental health is multifaceted, influencing everything from mood regulation and cognitive function to the management of mental health disorders. Understanding and harnessing the power of nutrition can be a pivotal element in maintaining mental well-being and facilitating recovery from mental health challenges.

### The Brain-Gut Connection

The brain-gut connection is central to the relationship between nutrition and mental health. It is a complex communication network linking the gastrointestinal tract and the brain. This connection means gastrointestinal distress can signal the central nervous system, potentially triggering mood changes. Similarly, the synthesis and functionality of neurotransmitters like serotonin, primarily generated in the gut and essential for mood regulation, may be influenced by the foods we eat.

## Nutritional Psychiatry

The discipline of nutritional psychiatry is a young one that focuses on how diet and supplements might help prevent and cure mental health conditions. Research suggests that eating a diet high in whole foods—vegetables, whole grains, seafood, and fruits—may lower the prevalence of sadness and anxiety. However, diets high in processed foods, sugar, and saturated fats have the potential to exacerbate these diseases. This data suggests that dietary modifications may be beneficial when incorporated within a holistic approach to mental health treatment.

## Essential Nutrients for Mental Health

Certain nutrients have been identified as particularly important for mental health:

**Omega-3 Fatty Acids**: Fish high in omega-3 fatty acids, such salmon and sardines, has been linked to a decreased risk of anxiety and depression. These acids play a critical role in brain function and neurotransmitter regulation.

**B Vitamins:** Vitamins B12 and B6, in particular, are vital for mood regulation and preventing mental fatigue. They produce and regulate neurotransmitters and can be found in meats, whole grains, and legumes.

**Magnesium**: Often called the relaxation mineral, magnesium has calming effects and is important for neurotransmitter function. It's in leafy greens, nuts, seeds, and whole grains.

**Zinc:** This mineral is involved in brain health and depression. It's involved in neurotransmitter and hormone production and is found in meat, shellfish, legumes, and seeds.

**Iron:** Iron deficiency has been linked to mood disorders and cognitive impairment. Iron impacts brain function and energy levels and are essential for the blood's oxygen transport system. Fish, poultry, red meat, and fortified grains are some sources.

### Dietary Patterns and Mental Health

There is a link between a decreased incidence of depression and the Mediterranean diet, vital in fruits, vegetables, whole grains, olive oil, and lean protein. Similarly, the Japanese diet, which emphasizes fish, vegetables, and fermented foods, is linked to lower rates of mental health issues. These diets not only provide essential nutrients but also minimize the intake of processed foods and sugars, which have been linked to poor mental health outcomes.

### Implementing Nutritional Changes

Incorporating nutritional changes into one's lifestyle requires a balanced approach. It's about making incremental changes rather than adopting a restrictive diet that could lead to deficiencies and stress. Improving the amount of natural foods you eat, drinking enough water, and consuming fewer processed meals and sweets can all help you feel better mentally.

However, it is important to consider nutrition as a part of a complete mental health treatment plan that also includes therapy, medication, exercise, and adequate sleep as needed.

The connection between diet and mental health demonstrates the body's interdependence. As research continues to unfold, it becomes increasingly clear that the food we consume plays a crucial role in maintaining physical health and supporting mental and emotional well-being. By embracing a balanced, nutrient-rich diet, individuals can enhance their mental health, improve their mood, and foster resilience in life's challenges.

The importance of sleep in maintaining and enhancing mental health cannot be overstated. Often likened to the body's reset button, sleep is critical in processing the day's experiences, healing from stress, and preparing for the challenges ahead. Neglecting sleep can profoundly affect mood, cognitive function, and overall mental well-being. Understanding and prioritizing sleep is crucial for anyone looking to maintain optimal mental health or recover from mental health challenges.

### Psychological Restoration

Sleep is a period of psychological restoration during which the brain processes emotions and experiences from the day. This processing is vital for emotional regulation and the consolidation of memories. Reduced coping abilities, elevated emotional reactivity, and trouble sustaining stable emotions can all result from sleep deprivation. Ensuring adequate sleep allows the mind to recover from the day's stresses and rejuvenate for the next day.

### Cognitive Function and Mental Health

There's a significant link between sleep and cognitive function. Sleep deprivation can impair attention, decision-making, problem-solving, and creativity. Prolonged sleep disturbances have been linked to a higher chance of mental health conditions like anxiety and depression. Conversely, improving sleep quality can enhance cognitive performance and reduce symptoms of these disorders, highlighting sleep's critical role in mental health maintenance and recovery.

### Sleep and Neurotransmitter Balance

Sleep impacts the balance of neurotransmitters in the brain, chemicals that regulate mood, alertness, and thought

68

processes. Disruptions in sleep patterns can alter these neurotransmitters, leading to mood swings, irritability, and even depression. Adequate sleep helps balance neurotransmitter levels, promoting stable moods and well-being.

**Stress and Sleep**

Stress and sleep have a reciprocal relationship. High-stress levels can make falling or staying asleep difficult, while poor sleep can increase stress sensitivity, creating a vicious cycle. Quality sleep is a buffer against stress, enhancing the body's resilience and ability to cope with stressors. Strategies to manage stress, such as mindfulness, relaxation techniques, and regular exercise, can also improve sleep quality.

**Strategies for Improving Sleep**

Improving sleep involves both lifestyle changes and the creation of a sleep-conducive environment. The body may be helped to recognize when to shut down by keeping a regular sleep schedule, reducing time spent on screens before bed, and developing a relaxing bedtime routine. The sleeping space should be calm, quiet, and dark for continuous sleep.

Those who suffer from sleep disorders, such as insomnia or sleep apnea, must seek professional help. Medical therapies for sleep apnea and cognitive-behavioral therapy for insomnia (CBT-I), which tackles the beliefs and behaviors that interfere with sleep, are two possible treatments.

**Sleep's Role in Recovery**

Prioritizing sleep is especially important for individuals recovering from mental health disorders. Sleep can enhance the effectiveness of other treatment modalities, including therapy and medication. Viewing sleep as an integral part of the recovery process encourages a holistic approach to mental health care, recognizing that physical health practices are deeply intertwined with mental and emotional well-being.

Sleep is a foundational aspect of mental health, influencing mood regulation, cognitive function, and the body's stress response. By prioritizing sleep and addressing any sleep disorders, individuals can significantly improve their mental health outcomes. Understanding the significance of sleep emphasizes the need for a comprehensive strategy for mental health that considers all aspects of wellness and emphasizes the close connection between the body's physical and cognitive needs.

# CHAPTER 9

## THE ROLE OF COMMUNITY IN HEALING

The role of community in the healing process is profound and multifaceted, underscoring the innate human need for connection, support, and belonging. As individuals navigate the challenges of mental health, addiction recovery, or the aftermath of incarceration, the support of a compassionate and understanding community becomes invaluable. This support system offers a network of care and resources and a sense of belonging that can significantly enhance the journey toward healing and recovery. In this exploration, we delve into how communities—formed by geographical proximity, shared experiences, or common goals—act as pivotal elements in nurturing resilience, fostering hope, and empowering individuals to rebuild their lives with strength and dignity.

## Finding Support Groups

Finding support groups is an integral step for many on their journey toward healing and recovery. These support groups offer a secure and encouraging space for people to talk about their struggles, victories, and experiences with like-minded people. The strength of support groups is in their capacity to dismantle barriers to isolation, promote a feeling of community, and provide consolation and hope to individuals in need.

Support groups are available in many different formats and address a broad variety of topics, such as mental health disorders, addiction recovery, living with disease, and reintegration following incarceration. The core principle that unites all support groups is the mutual exchange of support—a give-and-take that is both healing and empowering. Participants receive support and understanding from others and have the opportunity to offer the same, creating a reciprocal network of care.

The benefits of joining a support group are manifold. First of all, they provide a safe space for people to express their emotions in a sympathetic and nonjudgmental setting. Through this therapeutic expression, people can acquire insight into their coping or healing path and process their feelings. Support groups also provide practical advice and shared experiences, from navigating the complexities of mental health systems to valuable tips for maintaining well-being. This knowledge-sharing is invaluable, as it comes from lived experience and can often provide solutions and strategies that are directly applicable.

One significant benefit that support groups may offer is a strong sense of community and belonging. For many dealing with mental health issues or recovery from addiction, the feeling of isolation can be overwhelming. Support groups counter this isolation, reminding individuals that they are not alone. This feeling of unity and common goal may be very gratifying, increasing self-worth and cultivating an optimistic perspective on the healing process.

Furthermore, support groups often act as a bridge to other resources and forms of support, including professional counseling, therapy, and medical advice. They can recommend resources, guide people through healthcare systems, and encourage them to seek additional help.

Finding the right support group is crucial. It involves researching available groups that align with one's needs and preferences. Many support groups are specialized, focusing on particular issues or demographics, which can help individuals, find a community that truly understands their unique challenges. Additionally, with the advent of digital platforms, online support groups have become increasingly accessible, offering flexibility and anonymity for those who may not be ready for face-to-face meetings.

Participation in a support group, whether in person or online, requires openness and a willingness to engage. It's about creating a respectful and understanding environment by talking about your path and listening to others. For many, taking the first step to join a support group can be daunting, but it's a step that has the potential to transform lives.

Finding and participating in support groups is a powerful aspect of the healing process. These support groups offer a feeling of community, practical guidance, and emotional support that can help make the journey less lonely and more optimistic. People can get the support and understanding they need to deal with the difficulties of recovery and mental health by interacting with people who have gone through similar situations. This is because empathy and understanding are derived from having a common experience.

## Community Service as a Path to Healing

Community service emerges as a unique and impactful path to healing, offering individuals the opportunity to step outside themselves and contribute to the well-being of others. This act of giving back benefits the community and facilitates personal growth, healing, and a profound sense of fulfillment for those involved. People can find purpose in serving others, form meaningful connections, and connect with others via community service—all of which are crucial elements of the healing process.

The act of helping others has been shown to have a multitude of psychological benefits. It can significantly boost mood, enhance self-esteem, and reduce feelings of isolation. When individuals contribute to the welfare of their community, they often experience a sense of accomplishment and pride. This positive feedback loop reinforces their value and worth within the community, challenging any negative self-perceptions that may have been internalized due to past experiences or struggles with mental health.

Moreover, community service provides a sense of belonging and connection. Loneliness and isolation exacerbate anxiety and depression, two mental health problems. Meeting others who have similar interests and beliefs via community service initiatives promotes a sense of camaraderie and solidarity among participants. These social connections are vital, offering a network of support that can be leaned on during difficult times.

Community service also offers a unique opportunity for individuals to develop new skills and interests. Whether it's organizing events, mentoring youth, or working on environmental conservation projects, the tasks involved in community service can challenge individuals in healthy ways, promoting growth and learning. Skills development can boost confidence and provide a sense of competence and achievement.

For people suffering from addiction or reintegrating into society after jail, community service may be extremely important to their rehabilitation. It provides a constructive outlet for time and energy, reduces the risk of relapse by fostering a positive and proactive mindset, and helps rebuild trust within the community. By contributing positively to society, individuals can redefine their identity beyond their past mistakes, seeing themselves as valuable community members.

Incorporating community service into the healing process requires finding causes or organizations that resonate on a personal level. Aligning personal values with service activities enhances the overall impact and satisfaction derived from the work. It's also essential to approach community service with an open heart and mind, ready to learn from the experiences and stories of those you are helping. This openness can lead to profound insights and a deeper understanding of the shared human experience, further facilitating healing and growth.

Community service is a testament to the idea that healing is not just an inward journey but also an outward expression of compassion, empathy, and solidarity. It reaffirms the interconnectedness of all individuals and highlights the transformative power of service for those giving and receiving help. Through serving others, individuals find a path to recovery, discovering purpose, connection, and a more profound sense of belonging.

## Building a Personal Support Network

Building a personal support network is crucial in navigating life's challenges and fostering long-term mental and emotional well-being. This network, composed of friends, family, mentors, and peers, provides a foundation of support, advice, and encouragement. It's a safety net that catches us when we fall and a cheering section that celebrates our successes, big and small.

Creating a robust support network involves more than just surrounding oneself with people. It's about cultivating relationships with individuals who genuinely understand, respect, and care for you. These connections ought to be marked by empathy, trust, and a readiness to listen and provide assistance when required. The quality of these connections is far more critical than the quantity, as even a few close, reliable relationships can provide significant emotional support.

One key aspect of building a personal support network is openness. Being open about your needs, experiences, and struggles can be daunting, but it invites others to share their own, fostering deeper connections and understanding. Active listening and supporting others are also crucial, as strong relationships are built on reciprocity. Showing genuine interest in the lives of those in your network strengthens bonds and ensures that support flows both ways.

Diversifying your support network can also enhance its effectiveness. Different people can offer various types of support, perspectives, and solutions. For instance, a mentor or coach might provide guidance and advice, while a close friend offers empathy and a listening ear. Engaging mental health professionals, such therapists or counselors, may give a specialized layer of support by offering solutions and insights to address specific problems.

Maintaining and nurturing these relationships is just as important as forming them. Regular check-ins, expressing gratitude, and being there for one another during tough times are all practices that keep the network strong and resilient. Additionally, participating in community groups, clubs, or online forums related to personal interests or challenges can expand your network, introducing you to individuals who share your experiences or passions.

In the end, a personal support network is a dynamic and ever-evolving ecosystem of assistance that adjusts to your changing needs and circumstances rather than merely being a group of people. It emphasizes how crucial human connection is to recovery, development, and resilience and serves as a helpful reminder that we are not supposed to travel through life by ourselves. We offer ourselves a strong weapon for overcoming hardship and succeeding in all facets of life when we devote time and effort to creating and sustaining these connections.

# CHAPTER 10

## MAINTAINING MOMENTUM

**M**aintaining personal growth and recovery momentum is akin to keeping a steady pace in a marathon. After the initial burst of energy and determination, the challenge often lies in sustaining effort and enthusiasm over the long haul. This chapter delves into strategies for preserving progress, avoiding stagnation, and continuously moving forward, even when obstacles arise. It's about harnessing the initial spark of motivation and turning it into a lasting flame, ensuring that the path towards healing, growth, and self-improvement is not just embarked upon but faithfully traveled.

### Setting Realistic Goals

Setting realistic goals is like planning a journey with a map that guides you step by step toward where you want to be. Establishing attainable objectives keeps us motivated and focused, enabling us to translate our aspirations into deeds and successes. It's about knowing where you're headed, understanding the steps, and recognizing what you can achieve.

Start by thinking about what you want to accomplish. It could be improving your health, learning a new skill, or changing your personal life. Whatever it is, your goal should mean something important to you. This personal significance will keep you motivated when the going gets tough.

Once your objective is clear, divide it up into manageable chunks. If your goal is a long journey, these steps are like the rest stops along the way. They must to be clear-cut, doable assignments that get you closer to your end objective. For instance, walking for thirty minutes three times a week might be a step toward your health goals. These smaller steps are essential because they give you clear actions to focus on, making your larger goal seem less daunting.

Be honest about what you can achieve in a specific time frame. Setting a timeline can help keep you on track, but this timeline must be realistic. If you set deadlines too soon, you might get discouraged if you can't meet them. It's like planning to walk a mile in just a few minutes—it's not just hard, it's impossible for most people. Giving yourself enough time makes your goal more achievable and allows you to adjust your plan if things don't go exactly as expected.

Recall acknowledging and appreciating your accomplishments along the route. No matter how tiny a step you take, it's a win that gets you closer to your destination. Rewarding yourself for these victories boosts your confidence and shows how valuable your work is.

Finally, be prepared to learn and adjust. Sometimes, even with the best planning, things go differently than planned. A step you thought was doable is challenging, or you might face unexpected obstacles. That's okay. The key is learning from these experiences, adjusting your plan if needed, and moving forward.

Setting realistic goals isn't just about achieving what you set out to do; it's about growing and learning along the way. It's a process that teaches you about your strengths and limits and how to push beyond them. With each goal you reach, you'll find yourself more confident and ready to tackle the next challenge on your journey.

Creating a personal wellness plan is like drawing a map for your journey to feeling good, both inside and out. It's about deciding where to go with your health and happiness and then laying out the steps. This plan is unique because it's all about what works best for you. Here's how to make one:

**1. Start with Your Goals:** Think about what you want to achieve for your health and happiness. Do you want to feel more energetic? You can manage to stress better or get stronger. Your goals are like destinations on your map.

**2. Know What You Enjoy:** Your plan should include activities you like. Walking or hiking could be part of your plan if you enjoy being in nature. If music makes you happy, perhaps dancing or listening to uplifting songs could fit in. Sticking to a plan with things you look forward to is more accessible.

**3. Small Steps:** Break your big goals into smaller ones. To eat healthier, include one fruit or vegetable in every meal. Small steps are like little paths that lead to your more prominent destination.

**4. Make It a Routine:** Try to do your activities around the same time each day or week. This way, they become a regular part of your life, like brushing your teeth. When something becomes a habit, it's easier to keep doing it.

**5. Check-in With Yourself:** Now and then, ask yourself how you feel about your plan. Is it helping you feel better? Is there something you don't enjoy and want to change? It's okay to redraw your map if you find a better path.

**6. Ask for Support:** Share your plan with friends or family who can cheer you on. Knowing someone else is rooting for you can give you an extra boost to keep going.

**7. Celebrate Your Wins:** When you reach one of your smaller goals, pat yourself on the back. Celebrating your wins, big or small, can motivate you to keep moving forward.

**8. Be Kind to Yourself:** It's okay to have days when you don't stick to your plan. On those days, remember to treat yourself gently and give it another go tomorrow.

Creating a personal wellness plan is a fun way to care for you. By figuring out what you want, taking small steps, and being consistent, you're on your way to a healthier and happier you. And remember, your plan can always change as you discover new paths to wellness.

## Coping with Setbacks

Coping with setbacks is like dealing with bumps in the road on a long journey. Sometimes, things go differently than expected, no matter how carefully you plan. You might slip up on a healthy habit, face a tough day that throws you off track, or encounter an obstacle that feels too big to overcome. It's typical and inherent in the procedure. The important thing is not to let these bumps stop you from moving forward. Here's how you can cope with setbacks and keep going:

**1. Take a Deep Breath:** When you hit a setback, pause and take a deep breath. It helps calm your mind and lets you step back and see things more clearly.

**2. Be Kind to Yourself:** Show yourself the same consideration that you would a friend. Remember, everyone faces setbacks. They don't define your worth or the end of your journey.

**3. Look for the Lesson:** Every setback has something to teach us. Maybe you took on too much too soon, or life threw you an unexpected curve. Try to see what you can learn from the experience. This can help you plan better for the next time.

**4. Adjust Your Plan:** Sometimes, setbacks show us that our initial plan needs tweaking. Changing your goals, trying different strategies, or shifting your timeline is okay. Flexibility can be a key to long-term success.

**5. Reach Out for Support:** You can handle setbacks with others. Consult a support group, your family, or friends. Sharing your feelings can lighten your load, and others might offer helpful advice or encouragement.

**6. Celebrate Your Progress:** Look back and recognize how far you've come. Focusing on your progress can boost your motivation and remind you that one setback doesn't erase all the steps forward you've made.

**7. Start Small Again:** Getting back on track doesn't mean you must make a giant leap. Start with small, manageable steps. Little successes can rebuild your confidence and momentum.

**8. Keep Your Eye on the Prize:** Remember why you started this journey. Remembering your goals can help steer you back on course and fuel your determination to keep going.

**9. Practice Gratitude:** Even on tough days, there are things to be grateful for. Acknowledging these can shift your focus from what went wrong to what's going right.

Coping with setbacks is an essential skill on the road to achieving your goals. It's about never falling but about learning to get back up each time you do. With patience, resilience, and a positive outlook, you can overcome any bump and continue your journey toward success.

# CHAPTER 11

## COPING SKILLS FOR TRIGGERS AND CRAVINGS

Navigating the landscape of triggers and cravings is a critical aspect of maintaining progress in recovery from addiction or managing mental health challenges. These triggers—situations, emotions, or even specific people—can suddenly test one's resolve, sparking cravings or desires that threaten to undermine hard-won gains. This chapter delves into practical coping skills that can fortify individuals against these moments of vulnerability. By equipping oneself with a toolkit of strategies and insights, one can navigate through triggers and cravings with strength and resilience, preserving the journey toward healing and personal growth.

### Identifying personal triggers

Identifying personal triggers is like learning to read a map of your emotional landscape. It involves recognizing the specific situations, emotions, people, or environments that spark negative feelings or desires, especially those that might lead to unhealthy behaviors or relapse in the context of recovery. Understanding your triggers is the first step in developing effective strategies to cope with them, allowing you to navigate through challenges with greater awareness and control.

To identify your triggers, pay close attention to when you feel stressed, tempted, or unsettled. These feelings can act as clues, pointing towards potential triggers. It might be a specific time of day, place, or even people who bring about these emotions. Sometimes, triggers are connected to sensory experiences, like specific smells or sounds that remind you of past experiences.

Keeping a journal can be incredibly helpful in this process. Note down instances where you feel triggered, detailing the context, emotions, and the outcome. Over time, patterns will emerge, highlighting the common triggers that affect you. This self-awareness is crucial, as it turns automatic, unexamined reactions into conscious, understandable patterns you can address.

It's also essential to distinguish between external and internal triggers. External triggers are things outside you, like places, people, or situations. Internal triggers, such as thoughts, feelings, or memories, come from within. Both types can be consequential, but understanding this distinction can help better tailor your coping strategies.

Dialogue with trusted friends, family members, or a therapist can also reveal triggers you might not have recognized. Sometimes, others can observe patterns in our behavior or reactions that we overlook.

Once you've identified your triggers, you can work on strategies to manage them. This might involve avoiding specific triggers, developing stress-reduction techniques, or learning new ways to reframe your thoughts and responses. The goal isn't necessarily to eliminate all triggers from your life—that's often not possible—but to reduce their impact on you and enhance your ability to cope healthily and productively.

Understanding your triggers is an ongoing process; as you grow and change, your triggers might too. Regular reflection and adjustment of your coping strategies are essential to stay aligned with your goals and needs. Identifying your triggers empowers you to take proactive steps in your recovery and mental health journey, transforming potential obstacles into opportunities for resilience and growth.

## Creating constructive coping strategies

Creating effective coping strategies is crucial for overcoming obstacles in life and preserving mental and emotional wellness. Just as a gardener selects the right tools for tending their garden, choosing healthy ways to cope with stress, triggers, and emotional upheaval ensures you can nurture your well-being and grow through adversity.

Healthy coping mechanisms are strategies that help you deal with stressful situations or emotions in ways that are constructive and beneficial to your overall health. Unlike unhealthy coping mechanisms, which might provide temporary relief but often have long-term adverse effects, healthy coping strategies empower you to face your problems head-on, leading to lasting solutions and personal growth.

One key to developing healthy coping mechanisms is self-awareness. This involves understanding your emotional triggers, recognizing when you're under stress, and knowing how you typically react to such situations. With this knowledge, you can explore coping strategies that address your needs and preferences.

Exercise is a universally beneficial coping mechanism. The body releases endorphins during exercise, which are endogenous compounds that naturally elevate mood and reduce levels of stress hormones. Find a workout you love and include it into your schedule, whether it's a yoga class, brisk stroll, or dancing to your favorite music.

Two effective strategies for controlling stress and anxiety are mindfulness and meditation. These practices help you stay present in the moment, reducing rumination and worry about the past or future. Even in difficult situations, you may feel calm and clear by paying attention to your breath or practicing guided meditation.

Creative expression, through art, music, writing, or other creative outlets, offers another avenue for coping. These activities allow you to process and express emotions tangibly, providing a sense of release and satisfaction.

Building and maintaining strong social connections is also crucial. Talking about your feelings and ideas with close friends or family might help you feel better and provide fresh insight into your problems. Support groups, whether in person or online, offer the opportunity to connect with others who understand your experiences.

Finally, developing healthy coping mechanisms often involves setting boundaries and saying no to activities or obligations that add unnecessary stress to your life. Learning to prioritize your well-being and make time for activities that rejuvenate you is essential for long-term health and happiness.

Keep in mind that what works for one person might not work for another, so it's important to experiment with several approaches and determine which one best fits your needs. Creating effective coping strategies takes time, trial and error, and self-compassion. It's a personal process. By making an investment in this process, you give yourself the tools you need to handle life's obstacles with grace and resiliency, cultivating a sense of Well-being that penetrates every part of your existence.

## Contingency planning for high-risk situations

Contingency planning for high-risk situations is like having a safety net ready for when you walk a tightrope. It's about being prepared when you're most vulnerable to falling back into old habits or facing challenges that could disrupt your progress. This preparation involves identifying potential high-risk situations and having a clear plan of action to navigate them safely.

High-risk situations can vary widely depending on individual experiences, including stressful events, certain social settings, specific people, or even particular times of the year. The first step in contingency planning is to reflect on past experiences to identify these triggers. Understanding your high-risk scenarios is crucial for developing an effective plan.

Once you've identified potential high-risk situations, the next step is to outline specific strategies to manage them. This could involve a variety of tactics, such as avoiding particular triggers altogether, having a trusted friend on call for support, or practicing stress-reduction techniques like deep breathing or mindfulness. The key is to have a concrete set of actions that you can take to protect your well-being.

For instance, if you know that social gatherings where alcohol is present are a trigger, your plan might include:

- Bringing a non-alcoholic beverage to hold.
- Preparing a polite but firm way to decline offers of alcohol.
- Planning to leave early if you start to feel uncomfortable.
- Alternatively, avoid these gatherings altogether for a certain period.

Another essential element of contingency planning is to establish a support system. This could mean arranging for regular check-ins with a therapist, counselor, or support group, especially during periods you've identified as high-risk. Talking to someone may strengthen your dedication to your goals by offering emotional support and accountability.

It's also helpful to rehearse your plan mentally or through role-playing with a friend or therapist. Visualizing yourself effectively handling risky circumstances might make you feel more confident and equipped to handle genuine challenges.

Finally, contingency planning should include a response strategy for a setback. This might involve reaching out to a specific person for support, reminding yourself of the progress you've made and that one setback doesn't define your journey, and determining the steps you'll take to get back on track.

Contingency planning for high-risk situations is a proactive approach to maintaining progress in recovery or any personal growth journey. By anticipating challenges and preparing strategies to address them, you empower yourself to navigate through potential pitfalls confidently, keeping your long-term goals within reach.

# CHAPTER 12

## ADDRESSING STIGMA AND EMBRACING IDENTITY

**A**ddressing stigma and embracing identity are crucial steps in healing and self-acceptance. Stigma, whether it stems from society, within communities, or even internalized beliefs, can significantly hinder one's progress by casting shadows of shame and isolation. Conversely, embracing one's identity, with all its facets, allows for profound self-acceptance and empowerment. This chapter delves into the challenges of confronting stigma head-on. It provides direction on taking back and appreciating one's identity, encouraging pride and acceptance that opens the door to natural recovery and development.

## Social stigma's effects on mental health

Social stigma has a significant and widespread influence on mental health, making it more difficult to get treatment, find support, and make a full recovery. Stigma, essentially a mark of disgrace associated with certain conditions or behaviors, can come from societal attitudes, cultural norms, or even misconceived beliefs about mental health and addiction. It leads to people being labeled, stereotyped, and discriminated against, resulting in feelings of shame, isolation, and worthlessness among those affected.

One of the most immediate impacts of social stigma is the reluctance to seek help. Many individuals fear judgment not just from society at large but from friends, family, and employers. Their anxiety may keep patients from getting the assistance and care they require, which might postpone treatment and make their illness worse. The silence encouraged by stigma only furthers the gap in understanding and empathy, perpetuating myths and misconceptions about mental health and addiction.

Moreover, stigma can exacerbate the challenges of living with a mental health condition. Individuals may internalize societal judgment, leading to self-stigma, where they begin believing negative stereotypes about themselves. This can erode self-esteem and hinder the process of recovery, as individuals feel unworthy of help or believe that their condition is a personal failing rather than a treatable health issue.

The effects of stigma extend into various aspects of life, including work, education, and personal relationships. It can result in discrimination in the workplace, barriers to educational opportunities, and strains in personal connections, further isolating individuals and limiting their access to resources and support networks essential for recovery and well-being.

Reducing the effects of social stigma necessitates a diverse strategy. In order to debunk misconceptions and promote a more sympathetic understanding of mental health difficulties, education is essential. Sharing personal stories can humanize the experience of living with a mental health condition, breaking down barriers of fear and misunderstanding. Advocacy and awareness campaigns can also challenge societal attitudes, promoting a more inclusive and supportive environment.

Establishing safe spaces where people may ask for assistance and open up about their experiences without worrying about being judged is critical. These settings include online communities, therapy services, or support groups. Encouraging candid discussions regarding mental health in the workplace, in families, and in schools can also help move society toward acceptance and understanding.

Ultimately, addressing the impact of social stigma on mental health is about fostering a society where individuals are not defined by their conditions but seen as whole persons deserving of compassion, respect, and equal opportunities. It's about moving from judgment to empathy, isolation to community, and shame to dignity, ensuring everyone has the support and freedom to pursue healing and happiness.

## Self-advocacy and empowerment strategies

Empowerment and self-advocacy are crucial for overcoming stigma and embracing one's identity, especially when it comes to mental health and addiction therapy. These strategies involve understanding your rights, needs, and worth and taking active steps to communicate and assert these in various contexts. By becoming your advocate, you take control of your journey and contribute to changing the broader narrative around mental health and addiction.

**Understanding Your Rights and Needs:** Begin by educating yourself about your condition, treatment options, and rights, whether in healthcare, the workplace, or educational settings. Knowledge is power, and understanding your situation fully equips you to make informed decisions about your care and to challenge any misinformation or discriminatory practices you may encounter.

**Effective Communication:** It is essential to develop the ability to communicate effectively about your needs and experiences. This might involve preparing what you want to say beforehand, using "I" statements to express your feelings and needs clearly, and practicing active listening during conversations. Being able to articulate your experiences and requirements confidently can significantly enhance your interactions with healthcare providers, employers, and support networks.

**Setting Boundaries:** Establishing healthy boundaries is a form of self-care and advocacy. It's about knowing your limits and communicating them to others in a way that's respectful yet firm. This could relate to your time, emotional capacity, or the kinds of support you find helpful or unhelpful. Setting and maintaining boundaries protects your well-being and ensures your relationships are supportive and respectful.

**Building a Support Network:** A strong support network can be a tremendous asset in self-advocacy. Connect with friends, family members, or groups who understand your journey and can offer practical and emotional support. These relationships give you a safety net in trying times and enable you to speak out more successfully for others and yourself.

**Assertiveness Training:** Learning to be assertive (not aggressive) is a critical skill in self-advocacy. It's about expressing your thoughts and feelings confidently and standing up for your rights positively and respectfully. Assertiveness training can help you navigate difficult conversations, negotiate for your needs, and challenge stigma and discrimination.

**Empowerment through Education and Sharing:** Telling your experience may be an effective way to advocate and feel more empowered. By opening up about your experiences, you can challenge misconceptions, raise awareness, and inspire others. Additionally, participating in workshops, seminars, or advocacy groups related to mental health can further your understanding and provide platforms for engagement and change.

**Self-compassion and Positive Self-talk:** Cultivating a compassionate inner dialogue is a foundational aspect of self-advocacy. Replace self-criticism and stigma-driven narratives with affirmations of your journey's strength, worth, and validity. Self-compassion reinforces your resilience and empowers you to advocate for yourself with kindness and respect.

Self-advocacy and empowerment are dynamic processes that evolve with your journey. They require patience, practice, and perseverance but are deeply rewarding. Speaking out for yourself improves your well-being and helps foster a society where people who are undergoing mental health and addiction recovery are respected, understood, and supported.

## Creating a new narrative for personal identity

Creating a new narrative for your identity is a transformative process that allows you to redefine yourself beyond the constraints of past experiences, societal labels, or stigmas. This journey is about authoring a story that resonates with who you are and aspires to be, moving away from a narrative defined by others or past challenges. It's about embracing your strengths, values, and dreams and reflecting on how you see yourself and present yourself to the world.

### Reflect on Your Core Values and Strengths

Begin by reflecting on what matters most to you. What are your core values? What strengths have you leaned on through tough times? Identifying these can help you understand the foundations on which you want your new narrative to rest. Journaling, meditation, or conversations with mentors or close friends who may provide valuable insights into your character and development can all be used for this kind of introspection.

### Acknowledge Your Journey

Your past experiences, including struggles and triumphs, are integral to your story. Acknowledging them without letting them define you is crucial. This means recognizing the lessons learned and the resilience gained without allowing these experiences to limit your perception of who you can be. It's about shifting the focus from what happened to you to how you've grown and what you've learned.

### Set Intentions for Your Future

Envision the version of yourself you aim to become. What qualities do you want to embody? What achievements would make you proud? Setting intentions for your future helps steer your narrative in a direction that aligns with your aspirations. These intentions act as guiding stars, keeping you focused on your path of personal development.

### Embrace Positive Self-talk

The language we use to talk about ourselves shapes our identity. Adopting positive, empowering self-talk is essential in rewriting your narrative. Replace self-criticism and doubt with affirmations of your worth, capability, and potential. This positive internal dialogue reinforces your new narrative, helping to solidify your evolving identity.

### Share Your Story

When you're ready, sharing your new narrative with others can be a powerful affirmation of your identity. Whether through social media, personal conversations, or creative expression, telling your story on your terms allows you to own your identity fully. It also offers the opportunity to inspire and connect with others who may see reflections of their journeys in yours.

### Actively Live Your New Narrative

A new narrative is something you write or talk about; it's something you live. Align your actions with your values, strengths, and aspirations. Seek out experiences that reinforce your identity and contribute positively to your story. This could mean pursuing new hobbies, volunteering, or making career moves that reflect your passions and goals.

## Be Open to Evolution

Finally, understand that your narrative will continue to evolve. Your identity will naturally shift and expand as you grow, face new challenges, and achieve new milestones. Embrace this evolution as a sign of ongoing growth, and be willing to revise your narrative to reflect your continuous journey of self-discovery.

Creating a new narrative for your identity is a profound act of self-empowerment. It involves weaving your values, experiences, and aspirations into a story that truly reflects who you are and wish to be. If you take control of this story, you may navigate life with a fresh feeling of purpose, confidence, and authenticity.

# CHAPTER 13

## PROFESSIONAL SUPPORT AND THERAPY OPTIONS

Exploring professional support and therapy options marks a pivotal chapter in the journey toward healing and personal growth. This exploration acknowledges that while self-help and community support play significant roles in recovery, professional guidance offers specialized expertise and tailored strategies to navigate mental health challenges. This chapter delves into the various forms of professional support available, from traditional therapy and counseling to innovative treatment modalities. It aims to demystify seeking help, highlighting how professional intervention can be a cornerstone of adequate care, facilitating more profound understanding, resilience, and lasting change.

### Therapy modalities (CBT, DBT, etc.)

Exploring therapy modalities opens up a world of options for those seeking professional support for mental health challenges. Each modality or type of therapy offers a unique approach to understanding and addressing issues, allowing individuals to find a path to healing that resonates with their personal experiences and goals. Dialectical behavior therapy (DBT) and cognitive behavioral therapy (CBT) are two of the numerous choices that stand out for their wide application and efficacy.

CBT, or cognitive behavioral therapy, focuses on the connection between feelings, beliefs, and actions. Its basic tenet is that painful emotions and harmful behaviors can result from bad thinking patterns.CBT involves:

- Recognizing these mental processes.
- Challenging them.
- Changing them out for more sane and helpful ways of thinking.

This process helps individuals tackle problems more positively. With its practical techniques that can be used in everyday settings, cognitive behavioral therapy (CBT) is beneficial for treating a variety of disorders, such as anxiety, depression, phobias, and stress management.

## Dialectical Behavior

Therapy (DBT), a form of treatment that evolved from CBT, is particularly suited for individuals who experience intense emotions. Standard CBT methods for reality-checking and emotion control are combined with ideas of acceptance, mindfulness, and discomfort tolerance. DBT is especially effective for treating personality disorders, eating disorders, and for those who exhibit self-harming behavior. It emphasizes on providing patients with the skills they need to control their emotions, handle stress, and fortify their relationships with others.

Apart from CBT and DBT, there are several other therapy modalities, each with its unique focus and techniques:

**Psychodynamic** therapy explores how unconscious processes rooted in childhood affect current behavior and relationships. It's a deep dive into the self, aiming to uncover and understand deep-seated emotional pain and patterns.

**Humanistic** Therapies, including Gestalt Therapy and Person-Centered Therapy, emphasize personal growth and self-actualization. They focus on the individual's experience in the present moment and are grounded in the belief in human beings' inherent goodness and potential.

**Family** Therapy addresses issues affecting the health and functioning of families. It sees individual problems as part of a more extensive system and works on improving communication and relationships within the family unit.

Patients can talk about their issues in a supportive and safe environment with like-minded individuals during therapy. It provides a sense of community and belonging, which can be healing.

Choosing the suitable therapy modality depends on an individual's specific needs, personality, and the nature of their issues. To find the right match, looking into various therapy modalities or speaking with a mental health practitioner is usually helpful. The therapeutic relationship—feeling comfortable and connected with the therapist—is also crucial for effective treatment.

Exploring therapy modalities is a step toward understanding the breadth and depth of options available for support and healing. Whether through CBT, DBT, or another form of therapy, professional guidance can offer valuable insights and tools for navigating mental health challenges, fostering resilience, and promoting lasting personal growth.

## The importance of psychiatric care when necessary

The importance of psychiatric care, when necessary, is paramount in the landscape of mental health treatment. This specialized medical care focuses on diagnosing, preventing, and treating mental disorders, offering a comprehensive approach that may include medication management, psychotherapy, and lifestyle counseling. It's a crucial component for those who may need more than therapy alone to manage their mental health conditions effectively.

A broad range of mental health concerns are treated by psychiatry, including anxiety disorders, schizophrenia, and more serious mental illnesses such as bipolar disorder and depression. Developing a customized treatment plan that takes into account each patient's particular requirements is one of a psychiatrist's most significant responsibilities as a medical professional with specialized training in mental health.

One key aspect of psychiatric care is the ability to prescribe medications. For many people, these can be helpful in controlling symptoms, offering comfort, and raising quality of life. Medications such as antidepressants, antipsychotics, mood stabilizers, and anxiolytics can help balance brain chemistry and assist in restoring function. However, a comprehensive approach to treatment is typically achieved by combining medicine with other types of therapy.

Psychiatric care also involves a thorough assessment that can include physical exams, lab tests, and a detailed psychiatric evaluation. This comprehensive approach ensures that any underlying medical issues contributing to mental health symptoms are identified and treated. Furthermore, psychiatrists can evaluate the effects of medication over time, making adjustments as needed to optimize treatment outcomes.

The importance of psychiatric care extends to its role in providing crisis intervention. For individuals experiencing severe mental health crises, psychiatrists can offer immediate care, guidance, and referrals to necessary services, sometimes including hospitalization when needed for the safety and stabilization of the patient.

For many, seeking psychiatric care is a crucial step toward recovery and maintaining mental health. It's critical to understand that requesting this kind of care is a proactive move toward taking charge of one's mental health and a show of strength. The stigma that sometimes surrounds psychiatric treatment can deter individuals from seeking help, but it's essential to prioritize health and well-being over societal perceptions.

Psychiatric care plays a vital role in the comprehensive treatment of mental health conditions. Its importance lies in its ability to provide specialized medical evaluation and treatment, including medication management, to offer relief and support recovery. By understanding and embracing the role of psychiatric care when necessary, individuals can access the full spectrum of care needed to navigate their mental health journey effectively.

## Finding the right professional support system

Finding the right professional support system is critical in navigating the journey toward mental health and well-being. This involves seeking professionals who have the expertise to address your specific needs and with whom you feel a sense of trust and comfort. The right support system can significantly impact your recovery process, offering guidance, treatment, and understanding that resonate with your personal experiences and goals.

**Start with Research**

Start by learning about the many kinds of mental health providers, such as social workers, psychologists, therapists, counselors, and psychiatrists. Each brings a different approach and specialization, from medication management to various forms of therapy. Understanding the distinctions helps you determine which best suits your needs.

## Seek Recommendations

Seek referrals from relatives, friends, or dependable medical professionals who have had good experiences working with mental health specialists. Personal recommendations might help you launch your inquiry and provide you with a solid understanding of the demeanor and style of a professional.

## Consider Specializations

Numerous mental health practitioners have specific areas of expertise, such as trauma, substance misuse, depression, and anxiety disorders. Look for professionals whose expertise aligns with your specific challenges. Specialized care can be more effective, as it's tailored to address the nuances of your experience.

## Evaluate Compatibility

The therapeutic relationship is foundational to effective treatment, so finding a professional with whom you feel comfortable and understood is essential. To explore your requirements and learn more about possible therapists' communication styles and approaches, consider scheduling your first sessions with them. This is also an opportunity to ask about their experience, treatment philosophy, and what you can expect from the process.

## Check Credentials and Experience

Ensure that any professional you consider is appropriately licensed and credentialed in their field. It's also worthwhile to look into their professional background and areas of expertise. Many professionals have profiles online or information provided through their clinics that can give you insight into their qualifications and approach to care.

**Accessibility and Practical Considerations**

Consider things like accessibility, location, and whether they take your insurance or provide a sliding scale for payment. Accessibility can significantly impact your ability to maintain consistent care, which is crucial for progress.

**Trust your Instincts.**

Finally, trust your instincts. After meeting with a potential therapist or counselor, reflect on how you felt during the interaction. Did you feel heard and respected? Could you develop a trusting relationship with this person? For a therapy relationship to be successful, you and your therapist must feel at ease and trustworthy.

Finding the right professional support system may require time and patience, but the effort is well worth it. The right professionals provide expert guidance, treatment, and support and validate your experiences, empowering you to navigate the path toward healing and growth confidently.

# CHAPTER 14

## MAINTAINING MOMENTUM: STRATEGIES FOR LONG-TERM SUCCESS

For any personal development, healing, or recovery journey to be successful over the long term, maintaining momentum in the face of life's ups and downs is essential. This final chapter focuses on strategies to sustain progress, avoid burnout, and stay motivated over time. Whether navigating the challenges of mental health, overcoming addiction, or pursuing personal development goals, the journey is often marathoned rather than a sprint. Here, we explore practical approaches and mindset shifts that can help you maintain momentum, adapt to changes, and continue moving forward with resilience and determination.

### Realistic goal-setting and progress monitoring

The first stages in sustaining momentum toward long-term success are setting realistic objectives and monitoring progress.This process transforms lofty aspirations into attainable targets, providing clear direction and measurable milestones along your journey. Whether you're navigating mental health challenges, personal development, or recovery, these strategies ensure that your efforts are focused, motivating, and aligned with your ultimate objectives.

#### Setting Realistic Goals

**Break It Down:** Start with broad aspirations and break them down into specific, achievable goals. For example, rather than aiming for a general objective such as "enhance mental health," specify specific actions like "engage in mindfulness meditation for 10 minutes every day" or "attend therapy sessions twice a month."

**SMART Criteria:** Make sure your goals are Time-bound, Relevant, Specific, Measurable, and Achievable by using the SMART criteria. Your goals become clearer with the aid of this framework, which facilitates planning and execution.

**Flexibility:** Be open to adjusting your goals as needed. Life is unpredictable, and flexibility allows you to adapt to changes without losing sight of your overall direction.

**Tracking Progress**

**Keep a Journal:** Record your travels using a diary or an app on your phone. Journaling your thoughts, feelings, and actions can help you see where you're making progress and where you need to make adjustments.

**Celebrate Milestones:** Recognize and celebrate when you achieve milestones, no matter how small. This reinforcement can boost your motivation and commitment to your goals.

**Visual Aids:** Track progress using tools like charts, graphs, or vision boards. Seeing a visual representation of your achievements can be incredibly motivating.

**Seek Feedback:** Share your goals and progress with trusted friends, family, or therapists. External feedback can offer encouragement, perspective, and constructive criticism to help refine your approach.

**Reflect and Adjust**

- Periodically review your goals and progress.
- Reflect on what's working, what isn't, and why.

Make thoughtful modifications to your strategy using these insights to align with your changing requirements and situation.

Setting realistic goals and tracking progress are more than just planning and organizational tools; they're acts of self-care that acknowledge your journey's value and commitment to growth. By breaking down your aspirations into achievable steps and monitoring your trip, you empower yourself to navigate the path ahead with confidence, resilience, and a sense of purpose.

## Celebrating milestones in the recovery journey

Celebrating milestones in the recovery journey is an essential practice that reinforces progress and nurtures a positive outlook towards the future. Each milestone, whether days, weeks, or months of maintaining a goal or overcoming a particular challenge, is a tangible marker of your hard work, dedication, and growth. Acknowledging these achievements boosts your morale and strengthens your resolve to continue on your path.

**Recognize Every Achievement:** It's essential to acknowledge every success, no matter how small it may seem. From attending a therapy session to resisting a craving, each achievement is a step forward in your journey. Recognizing these moments can help shift your focus from the struggles to the progress you're making.

**Share Your Success:** Sharing your milestones with friends, family, or your support group can amplify the sense of achievement. It allows others to celebrate with you, encouraging and validating your efforts. This shared celebration can deepen your connections and remind you that you're not alone.

**Reward Yourself:** Create personal rewards for reaching milestones. These rewards should be meaningful and support your recovery. For example, if you get a six-month milestone, you might treat yourself to a day out in nature, a new book, or a wellness workshop. These rewards not only celebrate your progress but also reinforce positive behavior.

**Reflect on Your Growth:** Use milestones as opportunities to reflect on your growth. Look back on where you started and compare it to where you are now. This self-reflection may bring important insights into your areas of strength, development, and successful techniques.

**Set New Goals:** Celebrating a milestone is also a perfect time to set new goals for the next phase of your journey. New goals can keep you motivated and focused, ensuring that your recovery continues to move forward.

**Document Your Journey:** Consider maintaining a journal or creating a collage or timeline to show your accomplishments. This documentation is a powerful reminder of your resilience and capability to overcome challenges, encouraging you during tougher times.

Celebrating milestones in the recovery journey isn't just about marking time; it's about honoring the hard work, changes, and growth that occur along the way. These celebrations reinforce the value of your efforts, providing motivation and encouragement to continue striving toward your long-term goals. Never forget that every accomplishment is a sign of your strength and a step toward a better, happier version of yourself.

## Planning for the future with confidence

Planning for the future confidently is an empowering aspect of maintaining momentum on your journey. It's about setting your sights on the horizon, armed with the lessons you've learned and the strengths you've developed. This forward-looking mindset fuels your motivation and solidifies your commitment to continued growth and well-being.

**Reflect on Your Journey:** Start by reflecting on your progress and the obstacles you've overcome. This reflection grounds your plans in a realistic understanding of your capabilities and resilience. It reminds you that you have the tools and strength to face whatever comes next.

**Set Long-Term Goals:** Consider what you would like to see in the future. Think on several aspects of your life, including your work, relationships, personal growth, and health. Establishing long-term objectives provides you with a direction and something constructive to aim toward.

**Break down Your Goals:** Breaking down significant goals into smaller, more manageable steps might help prevent them from becoming overwhelming. This approach makes your goals more manageable and provides a clear path forward. It also allows for regular check-ins and adjustments as needed.

**Embrace Flexibility:** Developing a plan is important, but so is remaining adaptable. Since life may be unpredictable, it's important to be adaptable so you can deal with unforeseen developments without losing focus on your main objectives.

**Build a Support System:** As you plan for the future, consider the role of your support system. Embrace the company of like-minded individuals that support and believe in you. This network can provide advice, encouragement, and security as you progress.

**Invest in Personal Development:** Continuous learning and personal development can bolster your confidence as you plan for the future. Whether it's acquiring new skills, deepening your knowledge, or working on personal growth, these investments in yourself enrich your journey and open up new possibilities.

**Practice Self-Care:** Planning for the future means caring for your present self. Regular self-care practices ensure you are mentally, emotionally, and physically prepared for the future. Prioritize activities that nurture your well-being and keep you grounded.

**Visualize Success:** Spend time visualizing your future success. This powerful exercise boosts your confidence and motivation, making your goals more attainable. Visualization brings your future into the present, making it a tangible part of your journey.

Planning for the future with confidence is about more than having all the answers or a flawless roadmap. Instead, it's about trusting in your ability to navigate life's complexities, leveraging your strengths, and embracing growth opportunities. With a positive outlook and a strategic approach, you can chart a course toward a future filled with potential, ready to meet its challenges with resilience and optimism.

# CHAPTER 15

## THE ROLE OF SUPPORTED GROUPS AND COMMUNITY IN HEALING

Community assistance is essential when someone is trying to rehabilitate from issues connected to addiction or imprisonment. It encompasses a broad network of resources, including formal support groups, informal social support, and community-based programs, all aimed at providing the necessary scaffolding to help individuals rebuild their lives.

### Understanding Community Support

Community support refers to the help provided by various groups and organizations designed to aid individuals in recovery. This support can come from dedicated recovery groups like Alcoholics Anonymous, community centers offering educational workshops, or online forums that provide a space for sharing experiences and advice. The essence of community support lies in its ability to connect individuals with others with similar experiences and challenges, creating a network of understanding and empathy.

**The Role of Community Support in Recovery**

**1. Emotional Healing**

Community support groups provide a judgment-free environment where people can freely express their emotions and tell their stories. This sharing process is therapeutic and helps individuals process their feelings. For someone recovering from addiction, knowing others are facing the same struggles can significantly reduce feelings of isolation and shame.

## 2. Practical Assistance

Beyond emotional support, these groups often provide practical help, such as information about navigating public health systems, legal aid, or financial management tips. This practical guidance is invaluable for those recently released from incarceration as they adjust to their new life outside prison walls.

## 3. Accountability

Many community support programs incorporate systems of accountability, a crucial element for recovery from addiction. When old habits try to reemerge, accountability partners or group check-ins may gently prod people toward better choices and help them stay on track with their recovery objectives.

## 4. Social Skills Building

Engaging in community support groups helps individuals enhance their social skills through interaction and participation. These skills are often eroded after long periods of incarceration or addiction, and rebuilding them is essential for successful reintegration into society.

## 5. Access to Resources

Community groups often know about local resources, such as affordable housing, job training programs, and nonprofit healthcare that might be difficult for individuals to discover on their own. Access to these resources can be a game-changer in the recovery process.

## Benefits of Community Support

### 1. Reducing recidivism

For those recovering from incarceration, community support has been shown to decrease rates of recidivism significantly.

The social connections formed in support groups provide a network that can offer advice, job leads, and moral support, making a return to old patterns less likely.

## 2. Sustaining Recovery from Addiction

Support groups specific to recovery from substance use disorders, such as Narcotics Anonymous or SMART Recovery, provide ongoing support that is critical in sustaining long-term recovery. They offer a structured approach to dealing with addiction, including steps or principles that help individuals cope with the challenges of sobriety.

## 3. Enhancing Quality of Life

Community support can improve overall well-being and quality of life, helping individuals find meaning and joy beyond their recovery. Activities and volunteering opportunities within these groups can boost self-esteem and provide a sense of purpose.

## 4. Lifelong Learning

Many community programs offer workshops and classes to educate individuals on essential life skills, from managing stress to handling interpersonal conflicts. This education is crucial for personal development and can help individuals avoid triggers that might lead to relapse.

Community support is indispensable in the journey towards recovery from incarceration or addiction. It provides a multifaceted network that assists with emotional healing, practical aid, and social reintegration. For anyone on this path, engaging with community resources can elevate the recovery experience from merely surviving to thriving, offering tools and connections that pave the way for a fulfilled and balanced life. By leveraging the strength of community ties, individuals in recovery can find the support they need to maintain their progress and build a promising future.

## Alcoholics Anonymous (AA)

Alcoholics Anonymous (AA) stands as one of the most influential and widely recognized support organizations globally, mainly known for its success in aiding individuals struggling with alcoholism. Established in 1935 in Akron, Ohio, by Bill Wilson and Dr. Bob Smith, AA has expanded from a tiny local group to a global fellowship with more than two million members. This section explores the foundation, principles, functions, and the profound impact of AA on its members and society.

**Foundation and Growth**

Alcoholics Anonymous was established out of a desperate need to address the pervasive and misunderstood problem of alcoholism. The founders, Bill Wilson, a New York stockbroker, and Dr. Bob Smith, an Ohio surgeon, both suffered from chronic alcoholism and sought to create a support system that could sustain long-term recovery. They introduced the concept of peer support through shared experiences, strength, and hope, which later became the cornerstone of AA meetings.

The primary idea of Alcoholics Anonymous is that while sober people may support one another in becoming and staying sober, they cannot do it by themselves; a higher power and the community are essential. The group is widely accessible, non-professional, self-sufficient, multicultural, and apolitical. Everyone who wants to address their drinking issue may use it because there is no age or educational limitations.

**The Twelve Steps**

The Twelve Steps, a set of spiritual precepts meant to cause a "spiritual awakening" in adherents, are the foundation of Alcoholics Anonymous.

Here's a brief overview of these steps:

**1. Admitting Powerlessness:** Acknowledging that alcohol has taken control of one's life and that it is no longer controllable is the first step.

**2. Belief in a Higher Power:** Members think they may be made sane again by a force bigger than themselves.

**3. Decision to Turn Over Will:** The decision to put our faith and will in God, as each person perceives him.

**4. Moral Inventory:** Examining oneself with a keen and courageous moral eye.

**5. Admission of Wrongs:** Acknowledging the precise nature of our transgressions to God, oneself, and another person.

**6. Readiness to Remove These Defects:** Being fully prepared to have all of these flaws in character removed by God.

**7. Humbly Asking:** Humbly pleading with Him to erase our failings.

**8. List of Persons Harmed:** Enumerating everyone they had hurt and deciding to offer apologies to each of them.

**9. Making Amends:** Make direct reparations to such persons whenever you can, unless doing so will harm them or others.

**10. Continued Personal Inventory:** Maintaining their self-assessment and swiftly owning up to their mistakes.

**11. Seeking Through Prayer and Meditation**: Making an effort to deepen one's relationship with God as one gets to know Him via prayer and meditation, requesting only to know what His will is for us and to be given the courage to follow it.

**12. Spiritual Awakening:** Since these steps lead to a spiritual awakening, I am trying to share this message with alcoholics and apply these concepts to all part of my life.

## Meetings and Structure

The main focus of the AA program is meetings. There are private groups for alcoholics exclusively and open meetings that are open to friends and family. Meetings frequently involve group discussions when people share their aspirations, experiences, and strengths. This practice helps members cope with their struggles, learn from others' experiences, and continue practicing AA principles in their daily lives.

## Impact and Effectiveness

The effectiveness of AA is supported by numerous studies indicating that engagement with AA increases the likelihood of sustained sobriety. One of the strengths of AA is its widespread availability, with meetings held in over 180 countries and its literature translated into many languages.

## Personal Stories

The real power of AA often shines through in the personal stories of its members:

**John's Journey:** After years of struggling with alcoholism and multiple failed attempts at rehab, John found lasting sobriety through AA. His story reflects the typical journey of many who finally see hope and community in the rooms of AA.

**Emily's Empowerment:** Emily credits AA for her sobriety and helps her rebuild her life and relationships, showcasing the holistic recovery that AA supports.

Alcoholics Anonymous has proven to be a vital resource for countless individuals battling alcoholism. By fostering an environment of mutual support and understanding, AA helps people not only to quit drinking but also to learn how to live sober lives rich with new purpose and meaning. As AA continues to evolve, it remains a beacon of hope for many, embodying the principle of shared strength and communal healing.

## Narcotics Anonymous (NA)

The international, community-based group Narcotics Anonymous (NA) was founded in response to the unique requirements of that battling drug addiction. Founded in 1953, following the model established by Alcoholics Anonymous, NA provides a supportive network of peers who help each other stay sober through a program based on the Twelve Steps. This organization has been instrumental in assisting individuals to escape the cycles of addiction and rebuild their lives through shared experiences and mutual support.

### Foundation and Philosophy

Narcotics Anonymous was established due to the necessity for a support system tailored specifically for individuals battling drug addiction. The founders of NA recognized that the principles of the Twelve Steps could be adapted to address the unique challenges faced by drug addicts, promoting recovery and personal growth. The foundation of NA philosophy is the idea that addiction is a progressive, long-term illness that can be controlled but not cured.

### The Twelve Steps of Narcotics Anonymous

Similar to AA, NA's foundation is built upon the Twelve Steps, adapted to focus on addiction in general rather than specifically on alcohol. These steps guide members through self-examination, acknowledging weaknesses, making amends for harm done, and helping others with an addiction. The process fosters profound personal change, not only assisting members to abstain from drugs but also transforming their attitudes and behaviors.

## Meetings and Community Support

NA meetings are the organization's core activity and can be found in over 139 countries, with texts translated into 49 languages. Meetings provide a venue where people with an addiction can come together to share their struggles and victories in overcoming addiction. There are two types of meetings: "open," which is available for non-addicts to attend, and "closed," exclusively for recovering people with an addiction. These gatherings are essential for maintaining sobriety and offer a platform for continuous support and fellowship. Members share their experiences and gain insights into recovery, reinforcing their commitment to the NA program.

## Impact and Adaptability

The impact of Narcotics Anonymous is profound. Members often speak of the "miracle" of transformation from despair to hope and from isolation to community belonging. The adaptability of NA allows it to serve a diverse population, addressing various substances and patterns of addiction. This inclusiveness ensures that anyone who wishes to pursue a life free from drugs can find support and guidance within NA.

## Personal Recovery Stories

The true testament to NA's effectiveness comes from the personal stories of its members:

One member, Alex, describes how NA saved his life. He had reached the depths of despair due to his heroin use and found a new lease on life through the support and brotherhood found in NA. His journey from addiction to recovery highlights the personal transformations that are possible within the supportive framework of NA.

Sarah, a different member, talks about how NA assisted her in overcoming the stigma attached to drug use and recovery. Through the meetings, she not only found the strength to stay clean but also to rebuild her life and relationships that her addiction had strained.

Narcotics Anonymous plays a crucial role in public health by providing a free, accessible, and effective platform for recovery from drug addiction. The organization's emphasis on anonymity and one-on-one support fosters an environment where individuals can freely share and seek help without fear of judgment. As addiction continues to be a significant challenge globally, the role of NA becomes ever more critical. It is a pillar of hope and a source of strength for countless individuals striving to maintain sobriety and transform their lives. The enduring success of NA underscores the universal need for compassion, understanding, and community in the journey to recovery.

## SMART Recovery

With a focus on cognitive-behavioral methods and scientific concepts, SMART Recovery (Self-Management and Recovery Training) provides an alternative to conventional twelve-step programs like Alcoholics Anonymous (AA) and Narcotics Anonymous (NA). SMART Recovery was established in 1994 to provide a structured program that promotes self-empowerment and self-reliance to persons who are seeking freedom from addiction.

**Foundation and Principles**

SMART recovery is grounded in scientific research and uses a non-spiritual approach that contrasts with the spiritually-oriented twelve-step programs. Its methods are continually updated to reflect the latest advancements in scientific understanding, making it a dynamic and progressive option in addiction recovery.

**The Four-Point Program**

The framework of SMART Recovery is the Four-Point Program, which addresses motivation, craving management, emotion and behavior regulation, and lifestyle balance:

**1. Building and Maintaining Motivation:** Members are encouraged to identify their motivations for recovery and learn strategies to keep their motivation strong throughout the process.

**2. Coping with Urges:** The program provides practical tools to manage urges and cravings effectively, helping to prevent relapse.

**3. Managing Thoughts, Feelings, and Behaviors:** Participants gain emotional and behavioral control using techniques like Cognitive Behavioral Therapy (CBT), which corrects irrational thought patterns and establishes more effective coping mechanisms in the face of stress.

**4. Living a Balanced Life:** This point stresses the importance of creating a fulfilling and balanced life, which supports sustained recovery by encouraging healthy habits, enjoyable activities, and goal setting.

**Meetings and Structure**

SMART Recovery meetings are interactive discussions focusing on applying the Four-Point Program to everyday challenges. These meetings can be attended in person or online, providing flexibility and continuous support for individuals in recovery.

## Tools and Techniques

SMART recovery is renowned for its specific, actionable tools that aid in addiction recovery, including:

**Cost/Benefit Analysis:** This tool reinforces the benefits of sobriety by assisting users in weighing the advantages and disadvantages of their addictive habits.

**ABCs of Rational Emotive Behavior Therapy (REBT):** An essential tool for disproving and analyzing illogical ideas, which are the source of addictive behaviors.

**DEADS Strategy for Urges** is a set of strategies designed to manage urges creatively and effectively, helping individuals maintain control in critical moments.

## Impact and Effectiveness

Research has indicated that SMART Recovery is a valuable tool for managing addiction recovery. Its focus on empowerment aligns with modern therapeutic practices and appeals to those who prefer a scientific and secular approach to recovery.

## Personal Stories

The effectiveness and appeal of SMART Recovery are often highlighted through personal recovery stories:

**Tom's Journey:** Tom turned to SMART Recovery after his long battle with alcohol. Utilizing the program's tools, he was able to sustain his sobriety, rebuild his personal and professional life, and eventually guide others on their recovery journeys.

**Jenna's Path to Empowerment:** After overcoming opioid addiction, Jenna used the principles of SMART Recovery to maintain her sobriety. The program helped her avoid relapse and empowered her to support and mentor others.

SMART recovery provides a robust and scientifically supported framework for overcoming addiction. By emphasizing self-management, psychological resilience, and community support, SMART Recovery meets the needs of many who seek a more secular and empirically grounded approach to recovery. Despite shifting scientific understanding and recovery requirements, its ever-evolving techniques guarantee it stays applicable and efficient.

## Real-life success stories

The effects of support groups such as Alcoholics Anonymous (AA), Narcotics Anonymous (NA), and SMART Recovery are eloquently demonstrated by true success stories. These narratives highlight the organizations' methodologies and bring a human element to the statistics, showing the transformative potential of community and structured recovery programs.

**John's Rebirth:** John's battle with alcohol dependency spanned over a decade, characterized by several failed attempts at sobriety through various short-term programs. His turning point came when he attended his first AA meeting. Through the shared experiences and the twelve-step program, John found a supportive community that understood the challenges of addiction. The structured approach of AA, coupled with peer support, empowered him to maintain long-term sobriety. Today, John celebrates over fifteen years of sobriety and actively participates in AA meetings, now helping others as a sponsor.

**Lisa's Turnaround:** Lisa's journey into the world of narcotics started in her late teens. It wasn't long before her casual use spiraled into a full-blown heroin addiction, leading to multiple arrests and strained family relations. Lisa found a new hope through Narcotics Anonymous. The fellowship and the twelve steps helped her understand her addiction and provided a framework for recovery. By working the steps and forming close bonds with her group members, Lisa gradually reclaimed her life from the clutches of drug dependency. Three years clean, she now speaks at NA conventions and is a beacon of hope for newcomers.

**David's SMART Path:** David discovered SMART Recovery after his struggle with alcohol began affecting his professional life and personal relationships. Unlike AA, SMART Recovery's secular and scientific approach resonated with him, particularly its use of Cognitive Behavioral Therapy (CBT) and emphasis on self-empowerment. David used tools like the Cost/Benefit Analysis to weigh the benefits of sobriety against the allure of drinking and the DEADS strategy to manage urges. This rational and structured approach enabled him to overcome his addiction. Five years sober, David now facilitates a local SMART Recovery meeting, helping others navigate their path to recovery.

### Shared Themes across Stories

These stories share common themes of struggle, enlightenment, support, and transformation. Each narrative underscores the critical role these organizations play in not only helping individuals abstain from addictive behaviors but also in providing ongoing support that nurtures personal growth and recovery. John, Lisa, and David's stories highlight:

**Community and Support:** The strength in the community and the unique support provided by peers who have experienced similar struggles.

**Empowerment:** How self-help techniques and organized supervision enable people to take control of their healing.

**Transformation is the** profound personal growth that occurs through recovery, affecting all areas of life, from personal relationships to professional success.

These success stories are integral to understanding the full impact of recovery programs. They validate these organizations' methods, inspire others to seek help, and affirm that recovery, though challenging, is achievable and sustainable with proper support.

## The Fortune Society

An essential group that helps those leaving prison successfully reintegrate into society is the Fortune Society. Since its founding by David Rothenberg in 1967, the organization has expanded to become one of the most well-known in the sector, providing advocacy and various services to over 7,000 people annually. The Fortune Society's approach is holistic; it addresses not just the immediate needs related to employment and housing but also the deeper psychological, health, and social barriers that the formerly incarcerated face.

The organization's philosophy is rooted in the belief that every person deserves a chance to rebuild their life, regardless of their past. This ethos is reflected in every program they offer, from residential drug treatment facilities to alternatives to incarceration programs, education services, and supportive housing. Each initiative is designed to provide the tools and support necessary for individuals to transition into a productive, fulfilled life post-release.

One of the critical programs of The Fortune Society is its "Alternatives to Incarceration," which effectively serves as a powerful intervention to reduce the likelihood of recidivism. By offering educational workshops, vocational training, and individual counseling, this program helps participants develop skills and self-confidence. These services are critical for reintegration and empowering individuals to lead their communities away from cycles of crime and punishment.

The Fortune Society also strongly emphasizes advocacy, challenging the stigmas associated with former prisoners. They strive to shift public perception and policy, promoting more compassionate and practical approaches to criminal justice issues. This work includes lobbying for policy changes and providing public education to help communities better understand the challenges and potentials of formerly incarcerated individuals.

**Real-life stories from The Fortune Society**

**Michael's New Chapter:** After spending a decade in prison, Michael felt overwhelmed by the prospect of reentering society. The Fortune Society offered him not just a place to stay but a supportive community and access to critical training programs during his transition. Thanks to their assistance, he got employment, mended his relationships, and eventually utilized his experience to push for criminal justice reform. Michael's story is just one example of how The Fortune Society helps individuals turn their lives around, demonstrating the organization's commitment to transforming lives through community support and empowerment.

The Fortune Society serves as a beacon of hope for many returning citizens. Its comprehensive services not only address the immediate needs of the formerly incarcerated but also foster long-term stability and success. The organization's dedication to advocacy and policy change furthers its impact, making it a formidable force in the community's fight for justice and equity. Through its holistic approach and dedicated support, The Fortune Society continues to change lives and build futures for individuals looking to move beyond their past.

## Prison Fellowship

Prison Fellowship is an influential organization that focuses on spiritually rehabilitating incarcerated individuals through faith-based programming. Established in 1976 by Charles Colson, a formerly imprisoned advisor to President Nixon, Prison Fellowship has grown to be the most significant outreach organization in the country for inmates, ex-offenders, and their families. The organization believes that rehabilitation starts with spiritual renewal and aims to transform prisoners into responsible citizens.

Prison Fellowship provides inmates with various programs supporting their spiritual and personal growth. These programs include the Inner Change Freedom Initiative, a comprehensive, faith-based program that addresses inmates' spiritual, moral, and life skills needs. Other programs, like Angel Tree, support children and families of inmates during and after incarceration, helping to maintain family bonds and provide a network of support.

Along with advocating for justice reform, the group works to make the legal system more equitable and effective in rehabilitating inmates and facilitating their reintegration into society. Through these initiatives, Prison Fellowship aims to break the cycle of crime by restoring hope and purpose to those impacted by incarceration.

**Transformational Stories from Prison Fellowship**

**Carlos' Transformation:** Carlos entered the prison system with little hope for his future. Inside, he encountered Prison Fellowship's programs, which introduced him to new ways of thinking and living. The program's focus on spiritual growth helped him find peace and purpose, radically changing his outlook on life. Carlos participated in various workshops and eventually became a leader within the prison community, helping to mentor other inmates. Upon his release, Carlos used the skills and values he learned to become a community leader, advocating for criminal justice reforms and helping other ex-prisoners find their path to recovery. His story is a testament to the transformational potential of Prison Fellowship's programs—not only did they rehabilitate him, but they also empowered him to contribute positively to society.

**Jessica's Journey:** Jessica's life took a turn when she was convicted and sent to prison, leaving her young daughter behind. The separation was painful, but through Prison Fellowship's Angel Tree program, she was able to stay connected with her daughter. The program provided gifts on Jessica's behalf during holidays, keeping the bond alive. Beyond maintaining relationships, the program offered Jessica workshops that prepared her for life after her release. Through these initiatives, she gained spiritual growth and practical skills in parenting and job readiness. Upon re-entry into society, Jessica was better equipped to rebuild her life and make a stable home for her daughter. Her story highlights how Prison Fellowship's comprehensive approach supports the inmates and their families.

Prison Fellowship illustrates the profound impact that faith-based support and comprehensive rehabilitation programs can have on individuals affected by the criminal justice system. By focusing on spiritual renewal and practical skills training, the organization helps transform the lives of many often overlooked by society. The success stories of individuals like Carlos and Jessica underscore Prison Fellowship's programs' practical benefits and transformational potential. These narratives show the positive outcomes that can arise from such rehabilitative efforts and reinforce the importance of addressing incarcerated individuals' spiritual and emotional needs to foster genuine and lasting change.

# CONCLUSION

A s we journey through the landscape of personal growth and recovery, the tools and strategies we've discussed serve as beacons, guiding us toward resilience, understanding, and self-compassion. Recapping these essential elements underscores their significance in navigating life's challenges and embracing the path to well-being.

**Setting Realistic Goals and Tracking Progress:** We've explored the importance of defining clear, achievable goals and the power of tracking our journey toward them. This practice keeps us grounded in our progress, illuminates the path forward, and ensures our aspirations remain within reach.

**Celebrating Milestones:** Recognizing and celebrating each step of progress reinforces our motivation and affirms the value of our efforts. These celebrations nurture our sense of achievement and remind us of our capability to overcome obstacles.

Planning for the Future with Confidence: Looking ahead with optimism, grounded in a realistic understanding of our strengths and experiences, empowers us to set meaningful, long-term goals. This forward-thinking mindset encourages continuous growth and adaptability.

**Developing Healthy Coping Mechanisms:** We've highlighted the necessity of cultivating coping strategies that foster emotional and psychological resilience. Whether through exercise, mindfulness, or creative expression, these mechanisms enable us to navigate stress and challenges healthily.

**Contingency Planning for High-Risk Situations:** Preparing for potential setbacks with a clear plan of action ensures that we can face high-risk situations confidently and maintain our progress, even in the face of adversity.

**Identifying Personal Triggers:** Understanding the specific conditions or emotions that challenge our well-being allows us to address them proactively, minimizing their impact and strengthening our capacity for resilience.

**Building a Personal Support Network:** Being surrounded by a network of support provides a base of motivation, wisdom, and comprehension that is essential for maintaining momentum and creating a feeling of community.

**Self-advocacy and Empowerment:** Asserting our needs and rights, informed by understanding our worth and capabilities, empowers us to navigate our journeys with agency and dignity.

**Creating a New Narrative for Personal Identity:** By redefining how we see ourselves and our place in the world, free from the constraints of past experiences or societal labels, we open the door to self-acceptance and a more authentic expression of our true selves.

**Exploring Therapy Modalities and Professional Support:** Recognizing the value of professional guidance in addressing mental health challenges, from CBT and DBT to psychodynamic therapy, reinforces the importance of seeking specialized support tailored to our unique paths to healing.

Together, these tools and strategies form a comprehensive toolkit for anyone navigating the journey of personal growth, mental health, and recovery. They remind us of the strength within, the support around us, and the endless possibilities that lie ahead. As we move forward, let these insights be a source of strength, guiding us toward a future marked by resilience, fulfillment, and profound well-being.

Understanding that recovery is ongoing but manageable

Understanding that recovery is an ongoing process but entirely manageable is a crucial realization on the path to healing and growth. This route is not straight; instead it has curves and ups, like a winding path. Accepting this nature of recovery allows individuals to approach their journey with patience, resilience, and a proactive mindset.

Recovery, whether from mental health challenges, addiction, or personal setbacks, is a lifelong journey of self-discovery, learning, and adaptation. It involves continuously employing the strategies and coping mechanisms that work best for you and adapting them as your circumstances and needs evolve. The ongoing nature of recovery doesn't mean it's a relentless struggle. Instead, it's a testament to human resilience and the capacity for growth and change.

By segmenting the process into smaller, more reasonable steps and acknowledging each accomplishment, rehabilitation may be seen as doable. It means setting realistic goals, tracking progress, and being gentle with you when facing setbacks. It's about understanding and navigating your triggers effectively, continuously building and relying on a support network, and seeking professional help when needed.

Moreover, viewing recovery as manageable is about focusing on what you can control and letting go of what you can't. It involves cultivating a mindset of self-compassion, where you treat yourself with kindness and understanding, recognizing that perfection is not the goal—progress is. It's about finding balance and adjusting to maintain your well-being in various aspects of life, including relationships, work, and personal interests.

An essential part of managing recovery is staying informed and being open to learning new strategies for coping and self-care.

It might include exploring different therapy modalities, updating your wellness plan, or adopting new hobbies and activities that bring joy and fulfillment. It's also about advocating for yourself and prioritizing your well-being, ensuring that the decisions you make support your journey toward recovery.

Embracing recovery as an ongoing but manageable process fosters a sense of empowerment and hope. It turns life from being about getting by to actively directing it toward your values, objectives, and preferences. This knowledge promotes a proactive attitude toward problems and seeing them as opportunities for development and education.

Recovery is a continuous journey that is entirely manageable with the right mindset and tools. It requires patience, self-compassion, and persistence but rewards personal growth, deeper self-understanding, and a more prosperous, more meaningful life. By embracing this perspective, individuals can navigate their recovery with confidence, resilience, and optimism, knowing that while the journey may be ongoing, it is also filled with potential and promise. As we come to the close of this exploration into maintaining momentum and embracing the journey of recovery and growth, it's crucial to recognize the courage it takes to embark on this path. Your power and resilience are demonstrated by the actions you've taken, the difficulties you've encountered, and the advancements you've accomplished. Remember, the journey of healing and personal development is as unique as you are, and every step forward, no matter how small, is a victory.

It's essential to understand that setbacks are not failures but part of the learning process. They do not define your journey but offer invaluable lessons that contribute to your growth. The path may not always be clear or easy, but you can navigate it with perseverance, flexibility, and self-compassion.

Lean on your support network, cherish your connections, and remember you're not alone. Countless others are walking similar paths, each with stories of struggle and triumph. Sharing your experiences can lighten your load and inspire and uplift others on their journey.

Continue to set realistic goals, celebrate your milestones, and embrace the ongoing nature of recovery. Keep learning, growing, and adapting. Stay open to new experiences and perspectives, and allow yourself to be surprised by your capabilities.

Above all, be kind to yourself. Practice self-compassion and recognize the immense courage it takes to face your challenges head-on. Your journey is one of profound transformation, and each step you take shapes you into the person you are meant to be.

So, as you move forward, do so with confidence, knowing that you have the tools, the strength, and the support to continue on your path. Believe in yourself and your ability to overcome challenges. Your journey is a beautiful, ongoing process filled with endless possibilities and opportunities for growth.

Remember, the road to recovery and personal growth is not solitary. It's paved with the support, understanding, and shared experiences of a community that sees and values your efforts. Keep pushing forward, striving for balance, and embracing the journey with an open heart and mind.

Your experience is proof of the human spirit's unwavering resilience... Remember that each step, challenge, and triumph brings you closer to your true self and the life you wish to lead. Here to your continued success, resilience, and happiness on this journey.

# APPENDICES/RESOURCES

Creating lists of community resources and support groups is essential for anyone on the journey of healing, recovery, or personal growth. These sites offer crucial information, connections, and support that may be extremely helpful when navigating the opportunities and challenges associated with recovering from addiction, mental health concerns, or just trying to live a better life. An outline of the kinds of services and support groups you could think about adding to your list is provided below; however the specifics might differ somewhat based on your requirements and location:

## National and Local Mental Health Organizations

These organizations often offer various services, from help lines and online resources to local support group meetings. They may be helpful resources for learning about mental health issues, available treatments, and coping and wellness techniques.

## Online Support Communities

The internet has made it easier to find support communities catering to various needs and interests. Whether through forums, social media groups, or dedicated apps, online communities can offer 24/7 support, anonymity, and a vast network of peers and professionals.

## Addiction Recovery Groups

Organizations such as Alcoholics Anonymous (AA), Narcotics Anonymous (NA), and other specialist recovery groups offer structured support to those who are battling substance abuse and addiction.

. These support groups offer a framework for rehabilitation, a feeling of community, and shared experiences.

## Therapy and Counseling Services

Listing local therapists, counselors, and mental health clinics can guide individuals seeking professional help. Many communities have services on a sliding scale for affordability or offer specialized care for different demographics, including veterans, youth, and LGBTQ+ individuals.

## Educational Workshops and Seminars

Educational programs focused on mental health, wellness, and personal development can empower individuals with knowledge and skills for coping and growth. Local colleges, community centers, or mental health organizations might offer these.

## Crisis Intervention Services

Crisis hotlines and emergency support services are crucial for immediate help in severe distress or danger. Including national and local crisis intervention resources can provide a lifeline for those in acute need.

## Wellness and Recreational Programs

Programs focused on physical activity, mindfulness, art, and other recreational activities can offer therapeutic benefits and a positive outlet for stress and emotions. Community centers, gyms, and local nonprofits often host such programs.

## Legal Aid and Advocacy Groups

Legal aid organizations can provide assistance and advocacy for those navigating legal issues related to their situation, such as discrimination, disability rights, or access to care.

Creating and maintaining a list of these resources ensures that you, or someone you know, can quickly find support when needed. It's a living document that can be updated as you discover new resources or your needs change. Sharing this list can also help others in your community, fostering a network of support and information that benefits everyone.

## Worksheets for self-reflection, goal setting, etc

Worksheets for self-reflection, goal setting, and other personal development exercises are practical tools that can facilitate more profound understanding, clarity, and progress on your journey. By putting thoughts, feelings, and aspirations onto paper, you engage in a structured exploration of your inner world and external goals, creating a tangible record of your reflections and intentions. Here are some key types of worksheets that can support your journey:

### Self-Reflection Worksheets

**Gratitude Journaling:** A worksheet with prompts to reflect on daily or weekly moments of gratitude can enhance positivity and mindfulness.

**Mood Tracker:** A daily or weekly mood tracker can help identify patterns in emotional well-being, triggers, and the effectiveness of coping strategies.

**Thought Record:** This cognitive-behavioral tool helps examine and challenge negative thought patterns, promoting healthier thinking habits.

### Goal Setting Worksheets

**SMART Goals Template:** By helping you create goals that are Time-bound, Specific, Measurable, Achievable, and Relevant, this worksheet will help you make your goals more attainable and clear.

**Action Plan:** Divide your objectives into manageable chunks and include areas for setting due dates, jotting down resources needed, and monitoring your progress.

**Obstacle and Solutions Chart:** Identify potential challenges to reaching your goals and brainstorm possible solutions or coping strategies.

### Personal Growth Worksheets

**Strengths and Values Exploration:** Activities that help you discover your fundamental values and abilities so that your behaviors and goals align with your true priorities.

**Life Wheel:** To find opportunities for improvement, evaluate your level of happiness in a variety of aspects of your life, including relationships, profession, health, and personal development.

**Mindfulness and Self-Care Plan:** Create a personalized plan for incorporating mindfulness practices and self-care activities into your daily routine.

### Recovery and Healing Worksheets

**Trigger Identification and Coping Plan:** Recognize personal triggers and develop specific coping strategies for each, preparing you to handle challenges more effectively.

**Relapse Prevention Plan:** Outline strategies for maintaining recovery, recognizing warning signs of relapse, and planning steps to take in case of setbacks.

**Support Network Map:** Include your support system, including friends, family, professionals, and support groups, with contact information and notes on how each can provide support.

These worksheets can provide structure and direction to your self-exploration and goal-setting efforts. Regularly completing and revisiting these tools can offer insights into your progress, challenges, and changes, serving as a mirror and a roadmap. Remember, filling out these worksheets is as important as the answers you find, encouraging mindfulness, intentionality, and active engagement with your personal development.

**Reading list for further exploration on each topic addressed**

Creating a reading list for further exploration can deepen your understanding and provide additional perspectives on healing, personal growth, recovery, and mental well-being. The books listed below have been carefully chosen to provide insightful perspectives on the quest for a happier, healthier life. This list includes works on psychology, self-help, memoirs, and practical guides, providing a comprehensive resource for anyone looking to expand their knowledge and find inspiration.

**On Mental Health and Healing**

**1. "The Body Keeps the Score:** Bessel van der Kolk's ground-breaking book "Brain, Mind, and Body in the Healing of Trauma" examines how trauma impacts the body and mind and possible recovery strategies.

**2. "Feeling Good**: The New Mood Therapy" by David D. Burns explains how cognitive behavioral therapy (CBT) can cure depression and elevate mood.

**On Mindfulness and Self-Care**

**3. "Wherever You Go, There You Are** Jon Kabat-Zinn's book "Mindfulness Meditation in Everyday Life" This book provides helpful guidance on integrating mindfulness into everyday life while demystifying it.

**4. Jayne Hardy's "The Self-Care Project:** How to Let Go of Frazzle and Make Time for You" offers insights and activities for building a personalized self-care routine.

## On Personal Growth and Resilience

**5. "Daring Greatly:** Brené Brown's book "The Use of Vulnerability to Build a Brave, Meaningful Life is explored in the book "How the Courage to Be Vulnerable Transforms the Way We Live, Love, Parent, and Lead."

**6. "Grit:** "In her book "The Power of Passion and Perseverance," The formation of grit and its importance in attaining success are examined by Angela Duckworth.

## On Recovery and Addiction

**7. "Recovery:** Freedom from Our Addictions" by Russell Brand - Combines personal anecdotes with practical advice for overcoming addiction.

**8. "The Recovery Book:** Answers to All Your Questions About Addiction and Alcoholism and Finding Health and Happiness in Sobriety" by Al J. Mooney M.D., Catherine Dold, and Howard Eisenberg - A comprehensive guide to recovery from addiction.

## On Relationships and Support Systems

**9. "Hold Me Tight:** Seven Conversations for a Lifetime of Love" by Dr. Sue Johnson - Offers insights into forming more muscular, more fulfilling relationships through emotional connection.

**10. Rachel Wilkerson Miller's "The Art of Showing Up:** How to Be There for Yourself and Your People" guides readers through the development of meaningful relationships and support networks.

## Memoirs and Personal Stories

**11. "Educated" by Tara Westover** - A memoir about overcoming a challenging upbringing through education and personal resilience.

**12. "The Noonday Demon:** An Atlas of Depression" by Andrew Solomon - Combines personal narrative with in-depth research to explore the landscape of depression.

This reading list is a starting point for anyone exploring these topics further. Every book provides unique perspectives and methods to enhance your journey toward recovery, development, and well-being. Whether you're seeking practical advice, scientific understanding, or personal stories of resilience, a wealth of knowledge is waiting to be discovered.

As we reach the End of "Redemption Road: Navigating Mental Health and Self-Care after Incarceration or Addiction," we hope that the chapters within have served as a beacon of support and guidance on your journey toward healing and reintegration. Our mission is to illuminate paths to recovery and empowerment for those who have endured the challenges of incarceration or battled addiction. For instance, we share stories of individuals who have successfully reintegrated into society after incarceration and strategies such as mindfulness and self-reflection that have proven effective in their recovery. Each story and strategy shared here is designed to inspire resilience and offer practical tools for a fulfilled and balanced life.

This book is not just a collection of advice and experiences—it's a part of an ongoing dialogue about overcoming adversity and making meaningful life changes. Your journey is unique, and your insights are invaluable to us. We encourage you to engage with us, share your stories, and discuss how "Redemption Road" has impacted your path to recovery. Your input is essential to our ability to grow and assist those most need it.

Talk to us and tell us your story—what worked for you, what challenges you're facing, and how you're using the tools from this book in your daily life. Reach out to by leaving a comment below in the form of a review and we take each and every review/comment seriously. Every piece of feedback helps us make "Redemption Road" better and more responsive to your needs.

We are here to support you, to learn from you, and to grow with you. Let's keep the conversation going. We hope to hear from you soon. How can we make this book better? How can we make the journey smoother for you and others? Your voice matters—let it be heard. We sincerely appreciate your time and effort in sharing your stories and feedback, and we value your contribution to our community.

"In the tapestry of redemption, every thread of struggle weaves a story of resilience and hope. May your journey be a testament to the power of second chances and the boundless potential within."

With warmth and encouragement,

Entire Team @ Redemption Road

Made in United States
Troutdale, OR
01/06/2025

27654122R10076